ARTS SMART
The Creative Arts in Preschool

By Ann S. Epstein, PhD

HIGHSCOPE®

Published by
HighScope® Press

A division of the
HighScope Educational Research Foundation
600 North River Street
Ypsilanti, Michigan 48198-2898
734.485.2000, FAX 734.485.0704

Orders: 800.40.PRESS; Fax: 800.442.4FAX; www.highscope.org
E-mail: *press@highscope.org*

Editor: Jennifer Burd
Cover design, text design: Phire Advertising and Design, LLC
Production: Judy Seling, Seling Design
Photography:
Gregory Fox: Pages 1, 4, 7, 10, 14, 16, 19, 22, 26, 29, 30, 37, 38, 39, 41, 62, 66, 72, 75, 82, 94, 97, 101, 103, 104, 110, 159, 160, 172, 174, 176
Bob Foran: Pages 3, 5, 6, 8, 24, 42, 47, 50, 52, 56, 64, 84, 86, 88, 90, 108, 120, 129, 131, 132, 134, 150, 153, 166, 178, 187, front and back covers
Betsy Evans: Page 9
HighScope Staff: Pages 13, 18, 20, 23, 31, 48, 60, 69, 76, 80, 106, 114, 118, 122, 125, 136, 142, 144, 146, 162

Library of Congress Cataloging-in-Publication Data
Names: Epstein, Ann S., author.
Title: Arts smart : the creative arts in preschool / Ann Epstein.
Description: 1st edition. | Ypsilanti, MI : HighScope Educational Research
    Foundation, 2016.
Identifiers: LCCN 2015039923 | ISBN 9781573797429 (soft cover : alk. paper)
Subjects: LCSH: Arts--Study and teaching (Preschool) | Arts--Study and
    teaching (Preschool)--Activity programs.
Classification: LCC LB1140.5.A7 E679 2016 | DDC 372.5/044--dc23 LC record available at http://lccn.loc.
gov/2015039923

ARTS SMART
The Creative Arts in Preschool

Contents

Acknowledgments

With the publication of *Arts Smart: The Creative Arts in Preschool*, I have come full circle after 50 years in child development and early childhood education. From a lifelong interest in the arts, to investigating the development of creativity for my doctoral prelims and dissertation, to writing earlier publications about the arts for HighScope and the National Association for the Education of Young Children (NAEYC), this topic has been an ongoing theme in my work. Even when writing about other subjects, whether literacy, mathematics, or social-emotional and physical development, I have always recognized the importance of the arts in every area of early, and lifelong, learning.

Many people contributed their own interest in the arts, as well as their knowledge and skills, to the production of this book. I want to thank the entire staff of the Early Childhood Department at HighScope for their input and support. Special recognition goes to Christine Snyder, Shannon Lockhart, Holly Delgado, and Polly Neill for their creative activity ideas. Sue Gainsley thoughtfully reviewed the manuscript to guarantee that it was useful for teachers and engaging for young children.

Appreciation also goes to Editor Jennifer Burd and Editorial Assistant Nancy Goings, both of the HighScope Publications Department; Judy Seling, of Seling design, LLC, for the book design and layout; and to Gregory Fox, Bob Foran, and HighScope staff members for the photographs they contributed.

Finally, my thanks go out to all the artists whose creativity gives their own lives meaning and who inspire the rest of us to create the world anew every day. In other words, since we are all creative artists, thank you to everyone. Keep on filling the world with art, music, movement, drama, and an appreciation for the creative process that impels and sustains young and old alike.

PART I:
Introduction and Overview

This part of the book provides an overview of the importance of the creative arts, and how to effectively support the development of creative arts in young children.

Chapter 1 explains why the creative arts are important in early development and provides details about using this book.

Chapter 2 discusses the development of the creative arts in young children.

Chapter 3 offers general teaching strategies for supporting the creative arts in early childhood programs.

Introduction — Why the Creative Arts Are Important in Early Development

Humans have always used the arts to share and make sense of their deepest joys and fears. When we bring the shadows out of the caves and turn them into story, dance, song, or picture, we transform our emotions into something to share with others. And on those rare days when all the planets are perfectly aligned, we react in ways that lead to a greater understanding for all (Matlock & Hornstein, 2005, pp. 7–8).

The Benefits of Arts Education

Did you know that before becoming world famous scientists, Louis Pasteur was a promising young portrait painter in France, Charles Darwin was an avid photographer, and Albert Einstein played the violin every day? In fact, research finds a significant correlation between such high achievers in the world of science and involvement in the creative arts (Root-Bernstein, 2014). Not only Nobel prize winners, but patent holders and innovative business entrepreneurs also have in common that they engaged with art as children and continued to do so as adults (LaMore et al., 2013). Why does this connection show up time and again? Perhaps it is because those traits that characterize a scientist — the fine-motor

skills needed to pull a strand of DNA in the lab, a keen eye to observe minute differences, a fascination with materials, and the joy of building something from scratch — are rooted in the creative pursuit of art, music, dance, and dramatic play.

Despite clear evidence about the benefits of art education, many schools have reduced or cut it entirely from their budgets. Even early childhood programs, traditionally friendly to the arts, feel pressured to get children "ready" for kindergarten. Teachers spend time on literacy and math at the expense of meaningful art experiences. Fortunately, the backlash against a narrow focus on academics is restoring attention to the importance of social-emotional and physical development. The time is right to rally around the message that the arts are also vital in the early years.

This book contributes to the call to put art back into the early childhood curriculum. Although the book's main focus is on a set of activities adults can use to promote art, music, movement, dramatic play, and art appreciation in the classroom, the creative arts demand much more than providing materials or planning group times for children. Art is above all an attitude or spirit that values creative exploration and expression. Art thrives in an environment of serious play, respect for the artist, and recognition of the contribution that art makes to a vibrant and civil society.

The vision statement of the early childhood group of the National Art Educator Association begins, "Every child will have a quality early education in which rich and meaningful experiences in the arts are embedded" (2006, p. 20). Art educator Patricia Tarr (2008) says that embedding the arts goes even deeper than integrating them into the curriculum. Integration means that separate parts are combined into a whole. Embedded means enmeshed, or deeply rooted, in the daily life of the classroom, and includes looking at, making, and talking about art as an ongoing enterprise.

The creative arts introduce imagination and fantasy into the learning process — an "other world" as important to our survival as the "real world." The arts offer young children choice, control, and unlimited possibility, features

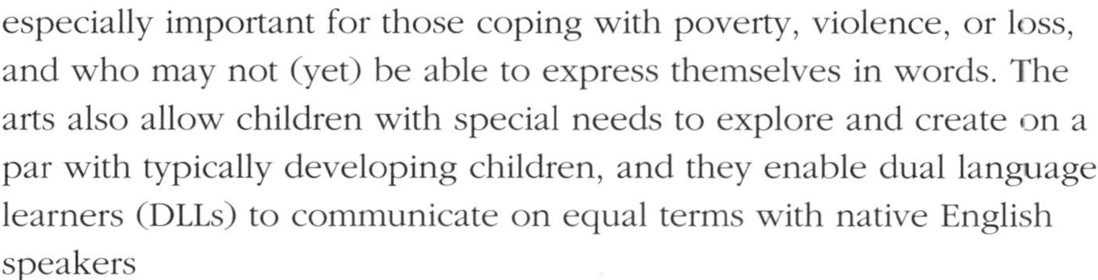

especially important for those coping with poverty, violence, or loss, and who may not (yet) be able to express themselves in words. The arts also allow children with special needs to explore and create on a par with typically developing children, and they enable dual language learners (DLLs) to communicate on equal terms with native English speakers

Educators speak of having a print-rich environment or one filled with numbers or nature. This book makes the case for an "arts-rich" life in which children establish an enduring belief in creativity as a human right. It proposes that the catch phrase for the domains of a comprehensive education should be "physical, social-emotional, cognitive, and *creative* development." Moreover, given the importance of the arts in the lives of scientists (as noted at the beginning of this chapter), the acronym STEM (Science, Technology, Engineering, and Math) should be expanded to STEAM, with the "A" standing for "Art."

Using This Book

The rest of this chapter briefly describes why the creative arts are important in and of themselves, and how they build knowledge and skills in other domains. Chapter 2 summarizes how the arts develop overall in young children. Then, completing Part 1, chapter 3 covers general teaching strategies to support the arts in the learning environment and daily routine, including sections on adaptations for children with special needs and those for whom English is their second language. In Part 2 of this book, Chapters 4 through 8 offer ten activities each, which are specific to each of the five areas that comprise the creative arts in the HighScope Preschool Curriculum: visual art, music, movement, dramatic (pretend) play, and art appreciation (Epstein, 2012; see "Creative Arts in the HighScope Preschool Curriculum" on p. 10). Before the set of activities for each area, you will also find developmental highlights, appropriate materials, and teaching strategies (with sections on diversity, special needs, and DLL). You can find an introduction to the activities at the beginning of Part 2, on page 37.

The Arts as a Distinct Content Area

When we view art as a distinct discipline, with a distinct body of knowledge that must be taught and mastered, we are not frightened to teach skills and techniques, as well as appreciation and art history. We will see art as an important discourse that should not be offered only to the special or talented, but as a universal and special way of making and communicating meaning, both at a personal level and in a broader sense as well (Wright, 2003, p. 154).

The creative arts serve three purposes in preschool education. They put young children in touch with their own senses, thoughts, and feelings; they allow children to express themselves in many ways; and they challenge children's ideas and help them make sense of the world around them.

Making and appreciating art allows young children to incorporate previous learning and connect it to new learning. The arts help children create meaning. "Meaningful learning engages feelings, experiences, relationships, and the ability to see clearly with our eyes, hands, and bodies" (Pinciotti, 2006, p. 11) — which is exactly what the creative arts do.

Working with art materials allows children to make their learning "visible" to others, both as a process and as a product. Children not only see and touch materials, they also "listen" to them — not just to the sounds but to the messages materials communicate: squeeze me, shake me, twirl me around, smear me across the page, turn me into a hat, use me to show that you feel angry.

In addition to promoting individual expression, creativity is often social. The arts can serve to connect children to adults and peers.

Renowned art educator Vivian Paley (1981) said that "trusting children with each other, without trying to control their discoveries, yields a richness rarely achieved when children work alone or under close adult supervision" (p. 11).

Finally, arts education should be offered to everyone, not just gifted children whose talent we want to nurture, nor disadvantaged youth who lack the resources to pursue the arts on their own. John Dewey (1934), the founder of progressive education, maintained that "the moral function of art itself is to remove prejudice" (p. 338). Because all cultures and most religions use art in their traditions and practices, art enables young children to integrate their cultural backgrounds into the school's curriculum (Wardle & Cruz-Janzen, 2004).

Art thus encourages an appreciation for diversity. The arts also smooth the inclusion of children with special needs. They allow them to participate fully in the life of the classroom, with or without specialized equipment, and enable all children to appreciate the talents and abilities of classmates (West, 2005). Likewise, children who cannot (yet) talk or who are learning English, can communicate with adults and peers through art. Images, sounds, and movements provide a universal language for sharing thoughts and feelings.

How the Arts Contribute to Development in All Areas

The arts invite children to imagine, solve problems, express ideas and emotions, and make sense of their experiences. Creative arts are a meaningful part of the early childhood curriculum for their own sake and because they can enhance children's development of skills in literacy, science, mathematics, social studies, and more (Koralek, 2005, p. 2).

Educators and researchers make a convincing case that the arts, and their underlying playfulness, should not be sacrificed for traditional school subjects. "Rather than diminishing children's learning by reducing the time devoted to academic activities, play promotes key abilities that enable children to learn successfully" (Copple & Bredekamp, 2009, p. xiii). For example, in high-level dramatic play, children have to **control their impulses** in order to collaborate, **remember** what went before to stay within the play theme, **use language** to communicate

their ideas, and **represent** objects and actions with props — capacities that are critical to later school success.

Some of the strongest data for how learning in the arts transfers to other areas comes from studies of brain development (Catterall, 2002a). For example, neural imaging shows that different regions of the brain are stimulated by different arts experiences (Sousa, 2006):

- Visual art excites the parts of our brain that allow us to recall or create fantasy.

- Music excites emotional areas. Melodic sounds produce pleasant feelings; dissonant noises, unpleasant ones. Music also stimulates the parts of the brain associated with mathematical reasoning. (However, listening to classical music cannot turn a child into a future Einstein!)

- Dancing activates the brain's motor neurons and spatial networks.

- Dramatic play turns on the neural networks that focus on spoken language and emotion.

- Art appreciation (using sensory cues to understand a work of art) enhances the brain's ability to form, retain, and recall memories.

Other research demonstrates a connection between experiences in the arts and children's well-being and achievement (Deasy & Stevenson, 2002; Horowitz & Webb-Dempsey, 2002). Studies consistently show that when the arts are part of the core curriculum, students are more task focused, persistent, cooperative with one another, and emotionally invested in learning overall. Creative, open-ended art activities

Creative Arts in the HighScope Preschool Curriculum

Key developmental indicators (KDIs) are those behaviors, observed in children's play, that reflect children's engagement with basic concepts and skills necessary for development. HighScope has identified 58 KDIs in eight curriculum content areas. The following are the KDIs for the Art curriculum content area.

40. Art: Children express and represent what they observe, think, imagine, and feel through two- and three-dimensional art.

Description: Children explore and use a variety of materials and tools to draw and paint, mold and sculpt, build and assemble. They use the properties of art materials (e.g., shape, color, texture) to represent their ideas. Children's representations and designs develop from simple to complex and from accidental to intentional.

41. Music: Children express and represent what they observe, think, imagine, and feel through music.

Description: Children explore and experience sound through singing, moving, listening, and playing instruments. They experiment with their voices and make up songs and chants. Children explore and respond to musical elements such as pitch (high, low), tempo (fast, slow), dynamics (loud, soft), and steady beat.

42. Movement: Children express and represent what they observe, think, imagine, and feel through movement.

Description: Children explore moving their whole bodies, or parts of their bodies, with and without music. They respond to the features and moods of music through movement.

43. Pretend play: Children express and represent what they observe, think, imagine, and feel through pretend play.

Description: Children imitate actions, use one object to stand for another, and take on roles themselves based on their interests and experiences. They use figures to represent characters in their pretend scenarios (e.g., having a "family" of toy bears talk to one another). Their play themes develop in detail and complexity over time.

44. Appreciating the arts: Children appreciate the creative arts.

Description: Children express opinions and preferences about the arts. They identify the pieces (e.g., a painting or musical selection) and styles they do or do not like and offer simple explanations as to why. Children describe the effects they and other artists create, and they develop a vocabulary to talk about the arts.

build executive function because they encourage children to plan, evaluate, and adjust their behaviors to reach a goal (Maynard & Ketter, 2013).

In sum, "the arts are not just expressive and affective, they are deeply cognitive" (Sousa, 2006, p. 20). The arts help young children enjoy the richness that creativity brings to everyday life, and assist them in developing the critical thinking skills and motivation they need to enter and succeed in school.

2

The Development of the Creative Arts in Young Children

Music, dance, drama, and story are the oldest ways human beings learned to pass on information, traditions, customs, and beliefs. Archaeologists have found instruments and pictures of dancers in caves. In the vocabulary of some Native American and African languages, there is no word for art, because art is part of everything the people do. Children are natural connectors. [They] see the arts as part of everything they do (Mimi Brodsky Chenfeld in an interview with Derry Koralek, 2010, p. 10).

Infants and toddlers connect to the world through their senses and movements. By preschool, children can use symbols to represent their understanding of people, actions, events, and ideas (Copple & Bredekamp, 2009). This growing cognitive ability expands their engagement with the creative arts as both "makers of" and "takers in." This chapter summarizes new research on the relationship between brain development and the arts, and presents an overview of children's development in making and appreciating art. Further details on early development in each arts area (visual art, music, movement, drama, and art appreciation) are presented in the activities in Chapters 4–8, respectively. For additional information on how young children develop their knowledge and skills in the arts, see also *The HighScope Preschool Curriculum: Creative Arts* (Epstein, 2012).

Brain Development and Creative Arts

The development of the brain influences how the young child engages with the creative arts. In turn, arts experiences affect brain development, with implications for how a child learns and performs in school. Put another way, perception, cognition, and affect are all deeply and profoundly interrelated. Therefore, as the emotional and thinking centers of the mind develop, they determine how children perceive and react to art. With infants and toddlers, experiences with visual stimuli, sounds, and movements will be primarily shaped by the affective and sensory parts of the brain. Although children this young do not of course recognize such input as art, they are nevertheless making neural connections about artistic elements such as color and form, light and dark, pitch, loudness, and the direction and speed of motion. For example, infants are born not only recognizing their mother's voice and their native language, they also respond more (wiggle, turn toward) melodies they heard often in the womb (Dewar, 2013).

As young children mature, the neural pathways that are formed, together with children's connections with earlier events and a growing ability to hold mental images in mind, affect experiences with the arts. For example, says arts educator James Catterall (2002a), the first time we hear a bassoon note, the part of the brain that deals with feelings signals whether we like it, the autonomous nervous system reacts to the sound, and the novelty of hearing it for the first time may trigger curiosity about how it was produced. The second time we hear it, the bassoon note stimulates neural pathways related to memory and recognition, and perhaps a higher level of cognitive analysis, such as comparing it to other sounds we have heard.

Different arts experiences also stimulate different parts of the brain, and thus affect early learning (Sousa, 2006). For example, music excites the auditory and emotional areas, producing pleasant feelings for melodic sounds and unpleasant feelings for dissonant sounds. Young children quickly learn to tell these apart. Music also

appears to affect the areas of the brain associated with mathematical reasoning, especially temporal and spatial relations. Dancing activates motor neurons and spatial networks; drama provokes neural networks that focus on spoken language and emotion; and visual art excites the systems that help us form, retain, and recall memories. Given these connections, it is not surprising that studies consistently find a link between early arts experiences and the development of social and academic knowledge and skills. The more children are exposed to the arts at a young age, the greater their emotional investment in learning, the higher their level of task focus and persistence, and the better they are at cooperative learning.

The Development of Making Art

The stages of artistic development do not have clear beginnings and endings (Taunton & Colbert, 2000). Children advance and retreat, much like adults artists do when they try out new materials or ideas. Nevertheless, research identifies four general progressions (Epstein & Trimis, 2002):

- ***From accidental or spontaneous representation to intentional representation.*** Younger children accidentally make something and then decide it looks like something else. This order is later reversed; children start with specific characteristics in mind and find materials or make movements to match their mental image. For example, a younger child will roll on the floor and say, "Hey! I'm moving like a ball!" An older child may say, "I'm going to be a ball. Watch me bounce up and down." Of course, at any stage, "happy accidents" can inspire creativity.

- ***From simple to elaborated models.*** Initially, children include one or two details in a drawing, song, movement, or pretend play scenario. Later, as they are able to hold more attributes in mind, their representations become more detailed. For example, a younger child pretending to be a baby may go "Waa! Waa!" in imitation of crying. An older child in the same role might wriggle and make faces, crawl, suck on a bottle, and/or reach out to be picked up.

- ***From randomness to deliberation.*** When children first explore an art medium, the sheer joy of touching, hearing, or moving is satisfying. Later, as they gain control over materials and tools, children's images and actions become more intentional. For example, lines and scribbles turn into shapes. Instead of making random sounds, children may try to reproduce a specific pitch (note), or replace disorganized movements with a deliberate circular or zigzag pattern.

- ***From unrelated elements to relationships.*** Children become increasingly aware of how marks, sounds, and movements relate to one another. Random marks that land on the page give way to lines that are connected. Single notes are strung together to make a tune. Mixing things together in a bowl leads to the idea of cooking and opening a restaurant. Aesthetics also begins to enter into the child's artistic decisions. For example, children place colors next to one another because they "look pretty together." Or they choose gliding to slow music over jiggling to fast music. These artistic preferences reflect their emerging ability to appreciate art.

The Development of Appreciating Art

Stages of art appreciation are often derived from the work of noted cognitive psychologists such as Jean Piaget (1926/1959) or Michael Parsons (1987), as well as from more recent work on how children construct knowledge (Bodrova & Leong, 2007). Although theorists may differ over the specifics, they typically describe children's aesthetic growth using three levels:

- ***Sensorial.*** The youngest children prefer abstract images and works that appeal to their senses. They respond to bright color contrasts and bold patterns, music with a strong beat, movements with a dominant action, and characters with clear personality traits. Children at this stage respond emotionally to art, and usually cannot explain why they like something, Often, one detail catches their attention to the exclusion of other aspects of the artwork. One form of art (for example, a painting) is interchangeable with another (for example, a photograph).

- ***Concrete.*** As children develop a sense for symbols, their preferences depend more on subject matter or theme. They like artwork that includes ideas they can relate to, portrayed in a simple and realistic manner. Children in this middle stage also develop an initial concept of beauty, again related to whether the subject matter appeals to them. They see the purpose of art as telling a "story" — through image, sound, or action — about real people and events. Children at this stage are also able to sort art within its medium (painting versus sculpture, string instruments versus horns, ballet versus jazz dancing), though not necessarily using the same terms as adults (for example, they may call all sculptures "statues"), and they have an understanding of time. Children can tell whether visual images, musical styles, or costumes are from long ago or now, or whether they are futuristic.

- ***Expressive.*** By late preschool or early kindergarten, children can begin to think about works of art from the artist's point of view — for example, what the artist was trying to express or why the artist chose a specific color, tempo, or movement. While older children still prefer realism, they show interest in subtle artistic effects and complicated compositions. They also become more aware of different artistic styles and how personal beliefs and culture affect an artist's work. Moreover, older children can explain and defend their artistic preferences.

From a developmental standpoint, it is clear that integrating the arts into the early childhood curriculum benefits a child's perceptual, physical, social-emotional, language, and cognitive growth. As an added value, studies consistently show that when art is part of the core curriculum, parents become more involved in their child's learning, teachers collaborate more when planning arts experiences, instruction is more active and hands-on, and child assessment is more varied (Sousa, 2006). Perhaps this is because parents and educators, regardless of their background, can themselves connect to the arts. They recognize the possibilities that the arts hold for young people's learning. As a result, this same research found, adults hold higher expectations for student achievement in all subject areas. In the next chapter, we look at general strategies for incorporating the arts into the preschool classroom and supporting children's involvement with the arts.

3

General Teaching Strategies for Supporting the Creative Arts

*Rather than focusing on the size or arrange-
ment of the classroom [to incorporate art],
the number one thing is spirit and the belief
that what you do is important. And we must
create a safe, loving, and trusting environment. It has to be part of your breathing, not
something you do only on Wednesdays* (Mimi
Brodsky Chenfeld in D. Koralek, 2010, p. 11).

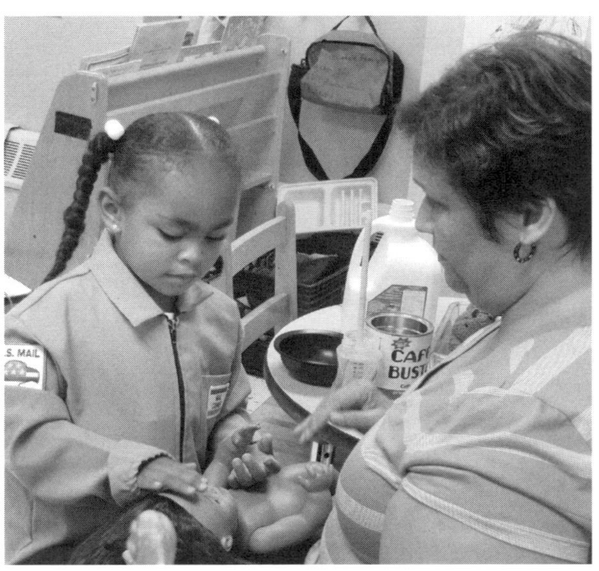

In describing developmentally appropriate
practices for the arts, Copple and Bredekamp
(2009) emphasize the importance of giving
children "daily opportunities for creative
expression and aesthetic appreciation"
(p. 175). This chapter explains the support
strategy of scaffolding and summarizes other
strategies teachers can use, when setting
up the learning environment and the daily
routine, to ensure that the arts are an everyday occurrence, not just an occasional event.
Ideas for incorporating multicultural diversity
into the arts curriculum are highlighted, and
there are sections on adapting materials and
activities for children with special needs and
dual language learners (DLLs). In addition to
the general arts strategies presented below,
specific strategies and adaptations are also
covered in the visual arts, music, movement,
dramatic play, and art appreciation chapters
that follow (Chapters 4–8). (For additional
information on teaching strategies that support the creative arts, see Epstein, 2012.)

Scaffolding

As adults employ various strategies to support children, they use scaffolding where appropriate. HighScope uses the term *scaffolding* to describe the process whereby adults support and gently extend children's thinking and reasoning. Scaffolding is a term introduced by developmental psychologist Jerome Bruner (1986) and is based on the work of psychologist Lev Vygotsky (1978). Vygotsky referred to the *zone of proximal development* as the area between what children can accomplish on their own and what they can do with the help of an adult or another child who is more developmentally advanced. High-Scope teachers carefully observe children so they know when and how to enter this zone. Children must be secure and confident in what they already know before they are ready to move to the next level. When HighScope says adults support and gently extend children's learning, it means that the adults first validate, or support, what children already know, and then, when the time is right, gently encourage them to extend their thinking to the next level.

For example, in the area of language and literacy, as children develop their vocabulary, a teacher might support a child by supplying the names of new objects or actions, such as *sphere* or *spin*. The teacher could gently extend the learning of a child who knows these words by adding descriptors — for example, "turquoise sphere" or "spin rapidly." In the area of the creative arts, to scaffold a child who is beginning to explore finger paint, a teacher might support the child by working alongside him or her, imitating what the child does with the material, such as dabbing it with a finger. To gently extend learning, the teacher could offer the child a tool, such as a sponge, to try together with the paint.

You will find specific scaffolding suggestions for each of the activities in Chapters 4–8 this book. These instructions, tailored for the particular activity in which they appear, can be found in a chart that is part of the instructions for the middle part of the activity.

Scaffolding Charts

You can also find charts of general scaffolding strategies for each of the five arts areas at the end of this chapter. Each chart describes what children at earlier, middle, and later stages of development may say and do, and how adults can scaffold (support and gently extend) children's learning at each level. Keep these overall strategies in mind and apply them to the specific activities described. For example, children at the earlier level may begin by exploring materials, especially if they are encountering them for the first time. Depending on the area and activity, exploring may consist of putting their hands in a puddle of paint, rolling a drum on the floor, or scrunching a streamer in their fist.

Supporting the Arts Throughout the Learning Environment

Use the following strategies to create a learning environment that encourages young children to explore the arts with curiosity, confidence, and a growing sense of control.

Provide opened-ended art materials and experiences.

Children thrive when they work with materials that can be used in diverse ways, and when they explore actions and ideas that build on their own interests. Non-art materials also help to develop the fine-motor, gross-motor, and eye-hand coordination skills that children can then apply to the creative arts. Having a wide variety of materials and tools, and the perceptual and motor skills to use them, allows children to execute their artistic ideas with more confidence and less frustration.

Educational consultants Walter Drew and Baji Rankin emphasize that open-ended materials and experiences allow children to connect the arts to their own lives. These connections make art meaningful and lead to authentic artistic expression and genuine creativity. As children sort, manipulate, and discover the possibilities of art materials, they act like scientists and engineers. "Key to this work is the teacher's respect for both the child and the materials. Open-ended materials are particularly effective because they have no predetermined use" (Drew & Rankin, 2005, p. 35). Providing interesting and diverse materials is not enough, however. Adults need to be intentional about engaging children with them and planning activities that help children discover and reflect on the cognitive and social possibilities embodied within the creative arts.

Establish a climate that supports creative risk-taking and emphasizes process over product.

Creating and appreciating the arts depends on having the freedom to explore and the confidence to take emotional risks. Children's artistic creativity thrives when the children feel supported and know they will not be judged for what they do and say. Treat their attempts to create something or voice an artistic opinion as learning experiences, never as failures. Don't praise work as being "pretty" or second-guess children's artistic choices or opinions — children may decide to play it "safe" in search of rewards, or they may refrain from expressing their views if they fear correction, disagreement, or ridicule.

To establish a supportive climate, emphasize efforts rather than results. You may need to gently explain to parents and school administrators why the demand to create a particular finished product is actually counterproductive. Resist pressures to put up "polished" artwork in the hallway or to send it home for the family refrigerator. Don't entice preschoolers to play "rehearsed" roles during performances staged for adults' amusement. Instead, point out what children learn when they explore materials, sing and move, and act out scenarios designed to satisfy only themselves and their own curiosity.

Draw on the artistic forms in the cultures of children's families and communities.

Before they arrive at preschool, children have encountered art in their homes and communities, and in the broader culture. So it is natural to integrate and expand their experiences in the classroom curriculum (Wardle & Cruz-Janzen, 2004). To deepen children's exposure, especially in ways that support their diverse backgrounds, include representative artwork from many media in the everyday furnishings, materials, and activities that make up your program setting.

There are multiple ways to bring art into the classroom, including displaying reproductions of fine art, incorporating different musical genres and movement styles in large-group activities and transitions, inviting community artists to visit or going to their studios, and taking field trips to galleries, museums, child-oriented performances, and public art displays. Contact local arts groups to find out what resources are specifically available for preschoolers, and work with their staff to make sure they know the interests and developmental levels of your children. Encourage families to share their interests and talents. They may be willing to loan artwork or recordings for use by the class. Encourage children to talk about where and how these things are used at home.

Supporting the Arts Throughout the Daily Routine

Planning specific activities for small- and large-group-time activities will help you be intentional about incorporating the creative arts into your program's curriculum. However, there are many other strategies

Work In Progress

When work time comes to an end, and children still have projects they'd like to complete, let them know they can place a work-in-progress sign on their creation, which lets others know it is not to be disturbed and that it will be worked on at a later time. The sign, which has the image of a hand with a slash through it, gives the message "Do not touch." Such a sign also helps children learn to use the concepts of "no" and "not."

you can use to guarantee that young children view the arts as part of everyday life. In addition to group times, try the following ideas as you greet and say goodbye to children, create a message board, help children plan, scaffold children's learning at work (choice) time, recall together, play alongside children outdoors, share meals and snacks, and help children transition to new activities.

Encourage children to represent real and imaginary experiences through the arts.

Young children represent familiar objects, people, places, and events through all forms of artistic media. They make drawings, imitate sounds and movements, and create pretend-play scenarios. While children naturally create art from these real and imaginary circumstances, their play and use of materials can actually be quite stereotyped and unvarying without adult support to extend it (Kindler, 1995). To help children expand their materials, actions, and ideas, try the following:

- At small-group time, reread a favorite book, and suggest children use the art materials you provide to create their own stories or ideas.

- At large-group time, provide opportunities for children to recreate familiar and imaginary movements (for example, big monsters with long legs). Play different types of music and suggest children move like various animals, depending on the volume or tempo.

- During transitions, encourage children to move to the next activity "as if" they were something or someone else (for example, a tricycle or a sleepy child).

- Take field trips to expand children's experiences, and encourage them to represent what they did, saw, heard, felt, smelled, and tasted.

- Take photographs of the children in the classroom and outdoors and talk about the sights, sounds, and movements that accompanied their activities. Encourage children to represent these during group times and by using the materials you provide at work (choice) time.

Building Blocks of the Daily Routine

The time segments of the HighScope daily routine designate a *process* or *place* rather than specific *content,* because the content is set by both children and adults. For example, here is how Mrs. Ballou, Mr. Andrews, and their children included movement experiences throughout their daily routine one day in the fall.

Greeting time — Max shows Mrs. Ballou how he climbed up the ladder into his new bunk bed. Mrs. Ballou and the other children imitate his actions — stretching, reaching, lifting their legs, and pretending to climb.

Message board — Looking at Mrs. Ballou's drawing, the children guess there is a new tricycle in the outdoor storage shed. "I know how to steer," says Gina, demonstrating with her arms.

Planning — Mr. Andrews and the group of children he plans with form a train and travel from area to area to have a look at all the choices before making their plans.

Working — The children in the house area have "sold" their "house." They fill a big carton so full of household goods that it takes all of them together to push it to their "new house."

Recalling — Mr. Andrews pats his knees to a steady beat and starts a recall chant: "I worked with the blocks today. This is what I have to say. I built them tall and that is all. Now it's Peter's turn to tell, what he did and did so well…."

Small-group time — Mrs. Ballou and the children in her small group use blocks to set up an obstacle course for the toy tumbling gnomes. She listens to children tell the gnomes where they should go and what they should do along the course: "Go up, up, up this side and then down to the bottom, right over here," Sophia tells her gnome.

Transition — After they put away their small-group-time materials, the children "tumble" like gnomes to the next activity.

Large-group time — Each child and adult has a capped plastic milk jug partly filled with water, which they swing, push, and carry in many different ways. Everyone seems to have a new idea to demonstrate.

Eating — Children exercise their fine-motor skills at snacktime as they pour their own juice, spoon out fruit salad, and pass the pitcher and the salad bowl to one another.

Resting — As children settle down on their cots, Mr. Andrews has them close their eyes and then quietly asks them to move their arms or legs like a gentle wind…like rain softly falling…like a bird flying home to its nest…like a little bear curling up for a long winter's nap.

Talk with children about the arts.

Many of the words children use to describe materials, sounds, and actions (such as *red, loud,* or *fast*) also apply to the arts. Encourage children to tell you, in their own words, about the art, music, movement, or pretend play scenarios they invent. While too many comments or questions can cut short a conversation, a well-timed remark or inquiry can lead to a satisfying exchange. Use thoughtful statements and divergent or open-ended questions that invite children to think about materials and actions, describe their choices, and reflect on the creative process itself (Burton, 2000). For example, you might say, "I wonder how you made that" or "What do you think makes this one sound louder than that one?" Children will learn that, in the arts, there is no such thing as "failure." Instead, artists simply try different solutions until they find one that pleases them.

Adaptations for Children With Special Needs

Creative arts should be an integrated component of *all* children's educational experiences. When we include children with differing abilities in art activities, they develop an appreciation for diversity in people as well as for materials and art forms (West, 2005). For children who cannot express themselves in words, art lets them say who they are inside and what they are thinking.

The objectives in an Individualized Education Program (IEP) can easily be embedded in creative activities. For example, visual art materials and tools promote fine-motor development and hand-eye coordination. Whole-body movement activities assist with gross-motor

development, such as balance. Singing enhances literacy, such as aural discrimination between sounds and syllables, while dramatic play supports language development, especially learning new vocabulary words. Children with special needs may also need more time to complete activities, so be sure to build this into your planning and scheduling. Encourage all children to help one another in getting out materials, executing their ideas, cleaning up, and transitioning to and from creative arts activities.

The following adaptations will not only maximize opportunities for children with special needs to be involved in art, many will also help typically developing children. Special educator Linda Crane Mitchell (2005) calls this making the MOST (materials, objectives, space, and time) of arts activities. You can just call it creative fun for everyone. (For additional ideas on adapting materials and activities for children with special needs, see Epstein & Hohmann, 2012, pp. 187–188. Also see area-specific adaptations in Chapters 4–8, respectively, in this book.)

Ideas for adapting materials

- Label materials with words and pictures.

- Encourage alternate ways to work with materials (e.g., provide rubber gloves for children who are oversensitive to texture).

- Stabilize materials to prevent slipping or falling (e.g., anchor easels, tape paper to table).

- Build in the use of communication devices (e.g., drawing apps on tablets, voice amplification for singing).

- Add visual, olfactory, and tactile stimulation (e.g., bright and contrasting colors in classroom furnishings; scented paint and play dough; different textures such as fabric swatches and small objects pasted into a storybook).

- Offer instructions in multiple formats, including visual (demonstrations, step-by-step pictures or photos) and verbal (explanations, step-by-step chants).

- Provide magnifying glasses, sound amplifiers, and other assistive devices.

Ideas for adapting space

- Create a dedicated art area with ample room for adaptive mobility devices.

- Allow room for children (with and without mobility aids) to work alongside one another.

- Acquaint children with spaces beforehand, and let them practice navigating the space.

- Provide movement and navigation cues with visuals, sign language, or braille.

- Add auditory or tactile cues to help children navigate (e.g., reflective tape, padded bumpers).

- Seat children with auditory or visual limits close to the teacher or materials being demonstrated.

- Raise or lower surface heights as needed (e.g., shorten table legs or add sturdy extensions).

- Provide alternative work surfaces that are accessible with wheelchairs (e.g., fold-out horizontal panels that extend from the wall over a child's lap).

- Use bolsters or pillows to prop children who have trouble sitting.

- Place bumpers or padding on walls and around the edges of large-motor areas and furniture so children needn't worry about banging into them with mobility devices.

- Remove or tape down rugs.

The Arts and Supporting Dual Language Learners (DLLs)

The creative arts serve a dual purpose for children who are dual language learners (DLLs). First, because the arts do not require language, they allow children to express their ideas and feelings through other media. For example, children can paint a happy picture, hum a sad tune, or pretend to cook their favorite foods. Second, participating in arts activities helps children whose first language is not English learn vocabulary words and syntax. The desire to communicate with their peers, whether to describe a painting they have made or take part in a pretend-play scenario, is a powerful motivator for trying out their language skills in a supportive environment. Teachers can use the following strategies to support DLLs through the arts.

Encourage children to communicate, regardless of which language they use.

The more children know their home language, the better their ability to learn a second language (Cheatham & Ro, 2010). Therefore, as DLL children engage in arts activities it is important for them to speak and write in whatever language(s) they can, and for teachers to acknowledge their contributions.

If you are not fluent in the other language(s) spoken by the children in your program, familiarize yourself with key words in those

languages that come up when talking about the arts. For example, learn common color and shape names, vocabulary for describing musical qualities such as *melody* and *tempo*, movement terms such as *jump* or *glide*, and the names of props or actions that typically appear in pretend play scenarios. When DLL children use these words, repeat them in the children's home language, and supply the corresponding English word. (Don't overdo it, but translate now and then when the child seems receptive.) When possible, pair non-English-speaking children with bilingual peers, to help the DLL children make the bridge with a companion who shares part of their identity.

To encourage language use in all its forms, sing songs, read books, and tell stories from children's home languages as well as English during group times. Encourage children to share familiar songs, fairy tales, and rhymes they hear at home, and to teach them to you and their classmates. These practices enhance the retention of the home language while contributing to learning English. Incorporating diverse musical and story sources also validates children's family languages and cultures, and helps monolingual peers recognize words and expressions used by DLL classmates.

Use pretend play to expand the vocabulary of DLL children.

Pretend play offers DLL children a chance to combine their emerging verbal skills with existing nonverbal abilities. For example, they can listen to or try out simple commands ("Put out the fire") while they wave a "hose" to douse the flames. Children who are native English speakers often fill in the words without DLL children having to ask, providing a natural learning opportunity. The structure and intonation of English,

which accompanies pretend play, also gives DLL children an occasion to learn more than just new vocabulary words. When teachers also partner with children during pretend play, they can further help them learn the vocabulary and structure of a second language.

Use narrative to enhance the fluency of DLL children.

Encourage DLL children to listen to stories and to tell their own. Listening to stories is a nonthreatening way to silently practice new and emerging English language skills. When they are ready to share stories, even if they don't yet have the English words, children can pantomime their ideas while you and other children fill in the missing vocabulary. Gradually, in stepwise fashion, DLL children will begin to try out their new language, first in combination with their native tongue, then mimicking familiar English words and phrases, and eventually expressing their own ideas in English (Tabors, 2008).

Don't think of narrative only in the traditional sense of reading or telling stories. Narration can happen at any time of the day. For example, a plan is a "story" about what children intend to do. Likewise, "recall" is a story about what they have done. Reading the message board is telling a story about what will happen that day. Children may also have stories to share at arrival time (what happened on the way to school) or just before departure (a special place they are going to after school that day). When adults describe what children do as they mold with clay, beat on a drum, or move to music, it gives them a "narrative" about children's actions and the materials they use to carry out their ideas. Working alongside children as the children make art and music, move in creative ways, or role play, also allows adults to draw out the children's personal stories and imagination.

In the end, the most important strategy to make the arts appeal to children of all developmental and ability levels and backgrounds is the attitude that adults convey. Words and actions "have the tremendous power to awaken the child to imagination, observation, investigation, exploration, planning, utilization, contemplation, and reflection with art materials" (Burton, 2000, p. 330). If you see art as essential to learning, you can confer these benefits on the children in your program. Then you can work beside them as you take off together in unexpected and exciting directions.

Ideas for Scaffolding KDI 40. Art

Always support children at their current level and occasionally offer a gentle extension.

Earlier	Middle	Later

Children may

- Explore the sensory properties of one or two materials (e.g., squish play dough; "The paint is cold").
- Use art and building materials in non-representational ways (e.g., stack blocks, smear finger paint, pound golf tees in Styrofoam).
- Work with materials and tools without being concerned about representing something (e.g., scribble lines, mold clay into blobs).

Children may

- Notice the effects created by materials or tools (e.g., using a wide brush; say "You can make fat worms with this brush").
- Make simple representations with one or two basic features (e.g., paint a circle with two dots for the eyes and a straight line for the mouth to represent a person; stack two blocks to represent a "tall house").
- Accidentally create an image and then recognize that it can represent something (e.g., roll clay into a log; say, "Hey! That looks like a snake").

Children may

- Use the properties (e.g., shape, color, texture) of materials or tools to represent something or create an effect (e.g., use a garlic press to make play dough hair).
- Make complex representations with several details (e.g., draw a person with a head, torso, legs, and arms; form a bowl with clay, fill it with balls as "berries," and insert a plastic spoon).
- Intentionally represent something (e.g., say "I'm going to make a dog" and draw a circle with four legs, a tail, ears, and facial features).

To support children's current level, adults can

- Work with materials alongside children.
- Imitate children's actions with materials and tools.
- Accept children's interest in exploring materials without trying to make something.

To support children's current level, adults can

- Comment on the effects children create with materials and tools (e.g., "A wide brush does make a fat line").
- Comment on the features in children's artwork (e.g., "You made a circle and put dots around the outside of it").
- Acknowledge that an image looks like what the child says it is (e.g., "That is round like the sun!").

To support children's current level, adults can

- Acknowledge when children create effects with materials and tools (e.g., "The garlic press makes the play dough look like hair").
- Talk about details children add to their artwork (e.g., "You mixed blue and green for the eyes. What about the hair?").
- Ask children what and how they will make something (e.g., "What will your dog look like? How will you make it?").

To offer a gentle extension, adults can

- Gradually introduce new materials and tools.
- Ask children to describe what they did so you can do the same thing (e.g., "Tell me how to make a mark just like yours.").
- Label simple representations yourself (e.g., refer to a ball of clay as a "meatball").

To offer a gentle extension, adults can

- Encourage children to anticipate the effects they create (e.g., "What do you think will happen with this brush?").
- Wonder what other details children could add (e.g., "I wonder what else you will add to your house").
- Model making and labeling something (e.g., say, "I'm going to make a spaceship and use these long pieces as the wings").

To offer a gentle extension, adults can

- Provide art vocabulary words for what children create (e.g., "Adding white made the blue a lighter tint").
- Encourage children to look at real objects and perhaps add details (e.g., a mirror if they want to add more facial features).
- Encourage children to represent their experiences (e.g., a field trip) at small-group time (accept if they choose not to).

Ideas for Scaffolding KDI 41. Music

Always support children at their current level and occasionally offer a gentle extension.

Earlier	Middle	Later

Children may

- Listen to sounds in the environment (e.g., stop what they are doing when a loud truck goes by); use classroom materials (e.g., pots, pans, car keys) to make sounds; attempt to copy sounds (e.g., siren of a passing fire engine).
- Observe (listen to) others singing; occasionally participate (e.g., babble along; sing a word or phrase); do a few accompanying movements.

Children may

- Label sounds (e.g., "That's the bell for cleanup time"); add sounds to the items they play with (e.g., car noises; doll baby cries); play different instruments.
- Sing simple familiar songs (e.g., "Row, Row, Row Your Boat"); sing all or most of the words to the refrain or chorus (e.g., "Jingle Bells" chorus); do most accompanying movements.

Children may

- Describe sounds in the environment (e.g., wind makes a "whooshing" noise; thunder goes "boom"; helicopter blades "whirr"); experiment with properties of sound such as fast/slow and loud/soft (e.g., tap a drum with different things to explore loudness; fill shakers to listen to the sounds made by different materials).
- Sing complex songs; sing chorus and verses; create and sing simple songs while they play (e.g., sing "Go to sleep baby. Go to sleep").

To support children's current level, adults can

- Call children's attention to sounds inside and outside the classroom (e.g., "Listen. I hear the train whistle"); imitate the sounds children copy (e.g., the sounds of toys, vehicles, and household items).
- Sing with children throughout the day; encourage them to participate but accept if they choose to listen.

To support children's current level, adults can

- Encourage children to name the sounds they hear; provide instruments that make a variety of sounds (e.g., tambourine, wood blocks, triangles, rhythm sticks).
- Include simple songs in the class songbook; ask children to choose what songs to sing (e.g., "Sonia, it's your turn to pick a song from the songbook").

To support children's current level, adults can

- Repeat the words children use to describe environmental sounds.
- Substitute words in songs; make up words to familiar tunes (e.g., to the tune of "Did You Ever See a Lassie," sing "It's time to do cleanup, do cleanup, do cleanup").

To offer a gentle extension, adults can

- Guess environmental sounds with children; provide sound-making materials for them to explore.
- Model and encourage children to sing one or two words such as where they will play (e.g., sing "Where are you going?" and they sing back "House area") or what they are doing (e.g., while they hammer, sing "Bing, bang, bing, bang").

To offer a gentle extension, adults can

- Introduce new vocabulary words to label sounds (e.g., *clang, whistle, hum, whoosh*).
- Gradually introduce more complicated songs and fingerplays during the year (e.g., songs with two verses or several movements).

To offer a gentle extension, adults can

- Comment on the sounds children create during play (e.g., "You made your train go 'clang'!"); encourage them to create other sounds (e.g., "I wonder what noise the baby will make in the bath").
- Encourage children to change words in familiar songs (e.g., "What else crawls up a water spout?") and to create songs (e.g., "How can we sing 'Put on your coat'"?).

Ideas for Scaffolding KDI 42. Movement

Always support children at their current level and occasionally offer a gentle extension.

Earlier	Middle	Later
Children may	**Children may**	**Children may**
• Explore moving their bodies or parts of their bodies. • Move their bodies independently of the features (tempo or mood) of the music (e.g., run fast to slow music).	• Use movement to represent their experiences in simple ways (e.g., flap their arms like a bird). • Move in one or two ways connected to the music (e.g., march to the beat; jump up and down to lively music).	• Use movement to represent their experiences in complex ways (e.g., twirl around and sway back and forth like a leaf blowing in the wind). • Describe how their movements are connected to the features of the music (e.g., "I'm moving slowly because this is floaty music").
To support children's current level, adults can	**To support children's current level, adults can**	**To support children's current level, adults can**
• Provide opportunities for children to move their bodies throughout the day in addition to large-group and outside time. • Play many types of music for children to move to; accept and encourage children to move in any way they want to the music.	• Imitate children's expressive movements (e.g., "I'm moving like a sad puppy, just like you"). • Describe your own and children's movements in relation to the music (e.g., "I'm tiptoeing when the music is soft"; "You're bouncing to the lively music").	• Describe children's complex movements (e.g., "You're crossing your arms and stomping hard to show how angry the monster is!"). • Provide a variety of musical features for children to move to (e.g., staccato, smooth, jazzy, waltz tempo; major and minor keys); describe the music and their own accompanying movements (e.g., "This is eerie music, so I'm creeping on the ground").
To offer a gentle extension, adults can	**To offer a gentle extension, adults can**	**To offer a gentle extension, adults can**
• Label their own and children's movements (e.g., "I'm flapping my arms"; "You're stretching"). • Imitate and describe how other children move to music (e.g., "I'm swaying to the music like Justin").	• Encourage children to move in a way they did at work time or during another recent activity. • Ask children to describe their movements and how they relate to the music (e.g., "What about the music makes you want to move that way?").	• Encourage children to move in an imaginary situation (e.g., "On our way to the rug, let's move like someone spilled glue on the floor"; "How would the Papa Bear move to the snack table?"). • Ask children to describe how their movements differ with contrasting musical styles (e.g., "How did you move differently when the music changed?").

Ideas for Scaffolding KDI 43. Pretend Play

Always support children at their current level and occasionally offer a gentle extension.

Earlier	Middle	Later

Children may

- Pretend to be a real person, animal, or object that is familiar to them from their own lives (e.g., crawl like a cat; whirr like a motor).
- Use an object to stand for another, similar object (e.g., pretend a small block is a cell phone).
- Engage in pretend play on their own (e.g., imitate truck noises while racing cars up and down a ramp; hold their arms out to the sides and "fly" like an airplane).

Children may

- Pretend to be a character in a story, song, nursery rhyme (e.g., the spider in Little Miss Muffet) or a generic role in a situation (e.g., a mom or dad feeding a baby).
- Talk in the "voice" of a character when playing with people or animal figures (e.g., use a high squeaky voice for a mouse); animate figures or objects (e.g., make an airplane fly).
- Engage in a simple pretend play scenario with another child (e.g., pretend to be horses together; pretend to be firefighters).

Children may

- Pretend to be a character or play a role they imagine (e.g., "I'm the daisy fairy who gives out flowers to sick babies").
- Create a prop during pretend play (e.g., scuba gear with tubing, milk jugs for oxygen tanks, safety glasses as swim masks, paper taped to shoes as flippers).
- Engage in complex play scenarios with others; step outside the role to clarify or give directions and then return to the play (e.g., say "Let's have the baby be sick. Marasol, you're the doctor. Okay, baby, mommy will take you to the doctor now," then rock and hand the doll to Marasol).

To support children's current level, adults can

- Pretend with children; imitate what they say and do (e.g., meow like a cat).
- Use a prop as a stand-in for the real object in the same way as the children (e.g., turn a plate like a steering wheel).
- Play in parallel with children.

To support children's current level, adults can

- Interact with children in character.
- Use figures similarly to children (e.g., create an animal family with figures; talk in a different voice with a puppet).
- Acknowledge when two children play together (e.g., at recall say, "Emilio, I saw you and Daryl being firefighters").

To support children's current level, adults can

- Allow extended time for children's detailed pretend play to fully develop.
- Provide materials to create props.
- Ask children to assign them pretend play roles (e.g., "Okay, I'll be the ambulance driver. Tell me what to do").

To offer a gentle extension, adults can

- Ask children what other features of real people, animals, and objects they can imitate (e.g., "What other sounds does your truck make?").
- Model using other materials to stand for or make familiar objects (e.g., "We could use this block for the table").
- Call children's attention to others who are pretending the same thing (e.g., "Jaron is racing his truck and going 'vroom' too").

To offer a gentle extension, adults can

- Encourage children to add details to their roles (e.g., "What else do dads do?").
- Gently try out other voices or actions for the figures but back off if children do not pick up on them (e.g., "My plane needs to land. I need to find an airport").
- Encourage children to describe their pretend play actions to others (e.g., "Daryl, can you show Pat how you and Emilio put out your fire?").

To offer a gentle extension, adults can

- Encourage children to imagine other scenarios (e.g., "What if there were no more sick babies for the daisy fairy?").
- Allow time for children to explore a variety of play options with the props they make (e.g., provide storage and work-in-progress signs; remind children of previous play at planning time).
- Provide consistent opportunities and materials for children to elaborate their play ideas over time.

Ideas for Scaffolding KDI 44. Appreciating the Arts

Always support children at their current level and occasionally offer a gentle extension.

Earlier	Middle	Later

Children may

- Choose without expressing an aesthetic preference; not state a like or dislike (e.g., pick the song on the first page of the song book; paint with blue because it's the color closest to them on the table).
- Observe or participate in the creative arts without paying attention to its artistic elements (e.g., look at a picture without commenting on its shapes or colors).

Children may

- Express an aesthetic preference but not be able to say why they do (or do not) like something (e.g., "I like the purple one"; "Twinkle, Twinkle is my favorite song").
- Describe one artistic element such as color or tempo (e.g., "It's red"; "That's fast music"); focus on the content rather than the style of the art (e.g., "It's a picture of a dog"; "Effie's pretending to skate").

Children may

- State a reason for their aesthetic preference (e.g., "Blue is my best color because it's like the lake where daddy taught me to swim"; "Not that book. The pictures are too scary! I like this one. The pictures are silly!").
- Describe several artistic features in terms of style and content (e.g., "It's a red circle with fuzzy edges"); say what their own artwork expresses (e.g., "This music makes me angry, so I'm stomping").

To support children's current level, adults can

- Accept that children may not have an aesthetic preference (e.g., "You like all three poems").
- Provide a variety of interesting artwork for children to look at and musical selections to listen to.

To support children's current level, adults can

- Validate children's aesthetic choices without making judgments or comparisons (e.g., "Some of us like to move to fast music and others prefer moving to slow music").
- Show interest in whatever artistic element catches the child's attention (e.g., "That is a big green square in the middle!"; "This music sure is fast!"; "Let's try to copy that movement together").

To support children's current level, adults can

- Acknowledge the reasons for children's preferences (e.g., "You like books with silly, not scary, pictures").
- Ask children to describe the content and style of their artwork (e.g., "Tell me about the lines you drew"; "What do you call it when you move that way?").

To offer a gentle extension, adults can

- Expose children to many artistic styles in a wide range of media so children can discover if/what they like.
- Comment on an observable characteristic of artwork or a noticeable difference in music (e.g., "There's a lot of yellow in this painting"; "This music is slow").

To offer a gentle extension, adults can

- Say why you do (not) like something (e.g., "I like this music. It makes me feel happy"); encourage children to say why they do (not) like something (e.g., "What makes you say this picture is yucky?").
- Refer children to one another to share observations (e.g., "Jeremy is looking at the same photo. I wonder what he sees").

To offer a gentle extension, adults can

- Provide a variety of artwork so children can find other examples of qualities they like (e.g., art reproductions; books by the same illustrator; music in similar genres).
- Expand children's vocabulary to describe materials, tools, techniques, and styles (e.g., "When the music is jumpy like this, it's called 'staccato'"); encourage them to describe what others are expressing in their artwork (e.g., "Why do you think the artist drew all these busy lines?").

PART II:
Activities

This part of the book offers 10 activities in each of five different content areas of the creative arts: Visual Art, Music, Movement, Pretend Play, and Appreciating the Arts. Together, these make up the Creative Arts content area in the HighScope Curriculum.

Chapter 4 offers visual art activities.

Chapter 5 offers music activities.

Chapter 6 offers movement activities.

Chapter 7 offers pretend play activities.

Chapter 8 offers arts appreciation activities.

Introduction to the Activities

The creative arts activities presented in Chapters 4 through 8 of this book can be used with preschoolers at different developmental levels. To make them meaningful for children with special needs and English language learners, see the general adaptations described in Chapter 3, and the specific suggestions for each of the five creative arts areas, found at the beginning of the activities

chapters (Chapters 4 through 8). To maximize cultural diversity, incorporate examples from the work of the artists and genres that are also given at the beginning of these chapters, and offer materials from the lists of materials used by artists in various cultures.

Structure of the activities

To help you implement each activity, the following information is provided:

Title of the activity: Each activity is numbered and has a short descriptive title.

Summary description: A short statement saying what the activity is about.

Time of day: The name of the part of the daily routine when the activity occurs. Most are designed for small-group time or large-group time, but there are also ideas for planning and recall times, transitions, snack- and mealtimes, outside time, and field trips.

Materials: The materials you need to carry out the activity, including materials for teachers as well as children. Generally, each person has his or her own set of materials but occasionally they are shared by the group or class. Sometimes the only "material" needed is the person's own body.

Curriculum content: The primary creative arts key developmental indicator (KDI) addressed by the activity; namely, visual art, music, movement, pretend (dramatic) play, or art appreciation. Additional area(s) of development or KDI(s) are also listed, if appropriate.

COR Advantage item: The primary COR Advantage item addressed by the activity. Additional COR Advantage item(s) that you may observe are also listed, if appropriate.

Beginning: A suggestion for introducing the activity to the children, usually with a brief statement or demonstration.

Middle: A suggestion for scaffolding learning during the activity, with an example at each developmental level — *earlier, middle,* and *later*). For additional ideas, refer to the scaffolding chart for that area, which you will find at the end of Chapter 3.

End: A suggestion for bringing the activity to a close, including giving children about a five-minute warning (more or less depending on how long it will take to clean up; you will want to allow more time for numerous or messy materials), putting away the materials together with the children, and using an aspect of the activity to help children transition to the next part of the daily routine.

Follow-up: A description of materials and subsequent activities to build on the children's experiences.

4

Activities for

Visual Art

It's not play dough. It's sculpture (preschooler quoted in Wien, Keating, & Bigelow, 2008, p. 78).

The Development of Visual Art in Children

Changes in virtually every aspect of development affect a young child's ability to create visual art. Cognitively, because preschoolers can hold images in mind — a flower, a person, the act of running — they can represent their observations and experiences in two and three dimensions. As children learn labels for attributes such as color, size, and texture, they use this knowledge when choosing and working with materials. Gains in social and emotional skills allow children to express their feelings in drawings, sculpture, and collage. Physical development, especially fine-motor skills and eye-hand coordination, enables children to use art materials and tools with increasing control.

Culture, as well as exposure, also influences the way young children perceive and create art. For example, some religions ban the use of the human figure in art and architecture. Instead, there may be more emphasis on geometric patterns or depictions of nature. Particular colors or design elements may predominate in various geographic or ethnic groups. Weaving or beadwork may be

common in one culture, carving or ceramics in another. Some children experience a great deal of art in their homes and communities; others see very little in their daily lives. All these factors can affect the young child's awareness of visual art in the environment, and his or her ability to make art. Despite these differences, researchers have identified a typical series of steps in developing art from late toddlerhood to the early elementary years (Swann, 2008; Wright, 2003):

- At first, children treat art materials as no different from other objects. For example, they may roll crayons, tickle their cheek with a paintbrush, or poke things into a lump of clay.

- Next children explore the properties of art materials and tools. For example, they discover that crayons make marks on paper, that the amount of pressure on a brush handle affects the type of marks the bristles make, and that clay can be patted flat, squished into a ball, or rolled into a tube.

- Children make simple representations, often accidentally (see Chapter 2), and name or label them according to some recognizable attribute. Thus a squiggly line may be a snake, blobs of paint may be called raindrops, and a flattened piece of clay may be identified as a pizza. Children will often describe their artwork in much greater detail than appears in the creation itself — for example, naming the "toppings" on the pizza even though the surface of the clay is smooth.

- Children become increasingly concerned with the accuracy of their representations, beginning with basic features and adding actual details. So a drawing of a snake may acquire thickness, a pattern

on its back, and a head with a darting tongue. Rain may fall in a scene that includes a house with a door and windows as well as trees and flowers. Items stuck in a clay pizza may include red beads for pepperoni or green confetti for peppers, and the pizza may even be cut into slices.

At every stage of creation, children are learning more about the nature of art and also about themselves. "Whether the intent is realistic depiction, storytelling, pattern making, or a combination of the three, children's visual intelligence is at work" (Soundy & Lee, 2013, p. 71). Moreover, for young children, drawing is also the first stage in learning to write. Visual art is a readily accessible language they can use to depict their experiences and express their ideas.

Materials and Equipment That Support Visual Art

Stocking the classroom and outdoor areas with the following equipment and materials will help preschoolers explore a variety of two- and three-dimensional art forms:

- Water source (indoor sink; outdoor spigot or hose)
- Smocks or paint shirts
- Sponges, towels, newspaper
- Surfaces including easels, walls, floors, wooden pallets, clipboards, pavement
- Fasteners (stapler, scissors, hole punch, glue, paper clips, elastic bands, pipe cleaners, string)
- Paper of various colors, sizes, textures
- Paints (tempera, watercolor, and finger paint in primary colors [red, yellow, blue], white, and black)
- Paint pumps
- Paintbrushes of various widths, with both flat and tapered ends
- Paint rollers
- Crayons (including a range of skin-tone colors)
- Colored pencils
- Markers of varying thicknesses
- Chalk, charcoal, oil pastels
- Ink pads and stamps, stickers
- Modeling clay
- Play dough

- Beeswax

- Sand

- Modeling tools (rolling pins, dowels, cookie cutters, tortilla press, garlic press, molds [containers] of various shapes and sizes)

- Collage materials (wood scraps, pieces of fabric, yarn, ribbon, feathers, beads, buttons, sequins, natural materials [shells, twigs, leaves, pebbles, pine cones])

- Frame loom, chainlink fence

For additional ideas on materials for the visual arts, see *The High-Scope Preschool Curriculum* (Epstein & Hohmann, 2012, Chapter 6 (pp. 171–221).

Teaching Strategies That Support Visual Art

To nurture and support young children's interest in visual art, use the following strategies as you carry out the daily routine:

Provide diverse examples of visual art throughout the learning environment.

In addition to painting and sculpture, help children become aware of the artistry in everyday objects such as a ceramic bowl, woven scarf, or hand-carved tool. Point out the beauty in nature, including the interplay of light and shadow, the many shades of green in the yard, or the design on the metal hinges of a door. Make sure that the examples of art throughout the room represent the diversity of children and families in your setting. For example, choose different types of fabrics and patterns in the dress-up area, and showcase artists from around the world in the book area.

Give children time to explore art materials and tools in depth.

While it is important to supply young children with a variety of open-ended art materials, don't overwhelm them with too many at once. Allow them to explore each material, by itself and then with tools, before introducing something new. For example, provide children with one primary color (red, blue, or yellow) with white and black, before giving them another color to mix in. Likewise, encourage preschoolers to feel and mold clay with their bare hands, over several days or across several small-group times, before you offer them a variety of modeling tools. When children are given the time to become familiar with a material, their ideas for using that material creatively expand.

Display and send home children's artwork.

Preschoolers enjoy sharing their artwork with others and seeing what their peers create. Set up wall space, shelves, and pedestals at the children's eye level to display their work. Encourage them to describe their creations to parents at dropoff and pickup times, emphasizing *how* the artwork was made rather than *what* the final product is. Let children take artwork home so parents can display it prominently and proudly.

For more information on teaching strategies that support visual art in preschool, see Epstein (2012, Chapter 3.)

Incorporating Cultural Diversity in Visual Art

Because art is a universal language, it allows people of different backgrounds to communicate with one another. Use online resources and those in your local library to discover more about visual artists whose histories are similar to those of the children in your program. Choose books with illustrations representing a wide range of artists and genres from around the world. Ask families to suggest artists or art forms they admire and/or whose work they have at home. Art is also a good vehicle for exposing preschoolers to people, settings, and cultural practices that differ from theirs. Find books and reproductions of artwork that illustrate different ways of life. Below are suggestions for diversifying the range of artists, genres, and media that children can encounter in the preschool setting. Build on these ideas to familiarize children with a wide range of visual art forms and the men and women who create them.

Artists. You might talk about and show examples of work by the following artists: Romare Bearden (African-American painter); Dawoud Bey (African-American photographer); I. M. Pei (Asian-American architect); Maya Lin (Chinese-American architect); El Anatsui (Nigerian collagist); Diego Rivera (Mexican muralist); Frida Kahlo (Mexican painter); Zaha Hadid (Iraqi-born architect); Isamu Noguchi (Japanese-American sculptor & landscape artist); Harvey Pratt (Native American painter and sculptor); Teri Greeves (Native American beadworker).

Genres. The following are genres you could introduce children to, which together reflect a diversity of cultures and influences: Chinese calligraphy; Japanese brushwork; Indonesian batik; Majolica pottery; Navaho rugs; African masks; African wood carving; Native American quill and beadwork; Native American sand painting; African quilts; Middle Eastern mosaics

Materials (media). You could introduce children to the following materials, which reflect artwork done in a variety of cultures: feathers; quills; beads; sand; charcoal; pen and ink; powdered minerals (nontoxic); wood blocks; tessera (mosaic tiles); yarn; raffia; embroidery thread; recycled (reclaimed and scrap) materials (cleaned and with rough edges or other hazards removed).

Adapting Visual Art Materials and Activities for Children With Special Needs

To enable children with a variety of special needs to participate fully in visual arts activities, try the following ideas:

- Provide alternate items that are easier to hold and manipulate (e.g., adaptive scissors, large paint brushes, glue sticks with velcro straps).
- Make brush handles and crayons easier to grip by wrapping them with masking tape or sliding them through a slit in a small rubber ball.
- Provide magnifying glasses and spot lighting (e.g., flashlights) to enhance visibility.
- Scent paints and play dough (e.g., with herbs and spices, cooking extracts) to provide additional sensory stimulation.
- Lower easels to make them more accessible.
- Strap boards for painting, drawing, and sculpting onto wheelchair trays.
- Buy hypoallergenic art materials.

Adapting Visual Art Materials and Activities for Children Who Are Dual Language Learners (DLLs)

Visual art does not depend on language, but it can be a vehicle to help children grow in their receptive and expressive English language skills. Try these suggestions with DLL preschoolers:

- Encourage children to name and describe, in their home language, the visual art materials and tools they use, and provide the English equivalent.
- Label visual art materials and tools in the language(s) children in the classroom speak, as well as in English.
- Encourage DLL children and native English speakers to collaborate during visual art activities, sharing their discoveries and ideas, and helping one another solve problems.
- Make "work-in-progress" signs in the language(s) children in the classroom speak, as well as in English.

- Partner DLLs with native English speakers during visual arts activities. Act as a translator to help children understand and carry out one another's ideas. Check with DLL children to make sure you have correctly understood and communicated their ideas. Check with native English speakers to make sure they understand the DLL children's intentions.

1

Collage Bin

Summary description: Children make collages from scrap materials they have gradually collected over time and saved in a classroom collage bin.

Time of day: Small-group time

Materials:

- Leftover and scrap materials children have deposited each day in a "collage bin" at cleanup time (things they find or bring from home, such as paper and fabric scraps, crayons stubs, bits of dried play dough, pieces of string)
- Supplementary scrap materials as needed (e.g., wood scraps, yarn, netting)

- Sheets of construction paper, cardboard, or other sturdy paper on which to make the collages
- Fasteners such as tape and glue
- Damp sponges and paper towels for wiping up drips and spills

Curriculum content: KDI 40. Art.
Also: KDI 17. Fine-motor skills

COR Advantage item: X. Art.
Also: item J. Fine-motor skills

Beginning: Tell the children that today they are going to make collages using the materials the class has been collecting in the collage bin. Give each child a piece of paper and a small basket of materials and glue or tape.

Middle: Circulate among the children, talking about the materials they are using and how they are arranging and fastening (sticking) them to their paper. Describe — and encourage children to describe — the materials' attributes, such as color, shape, size, and texture. Put the remaining scrap materials, along with the fasteners, in the middle of the table for the group to share. Describe children's work and encourage them to look at and comment on one another's work; for example, you might say, "I see you made a shiny collage by gluing foil onto your paper." Help the children solve problems as they arise — for example, difficulties getting certain materials to stick to the page.

The chart at right offers an example, at each developmental level, of what children may say and do, along with ideas for scaffolding (supporting and gently extending) their learning. For additional ideas, refer to the scaffolding chart for Art on page 32. To read more about scaffolding, see page 20.

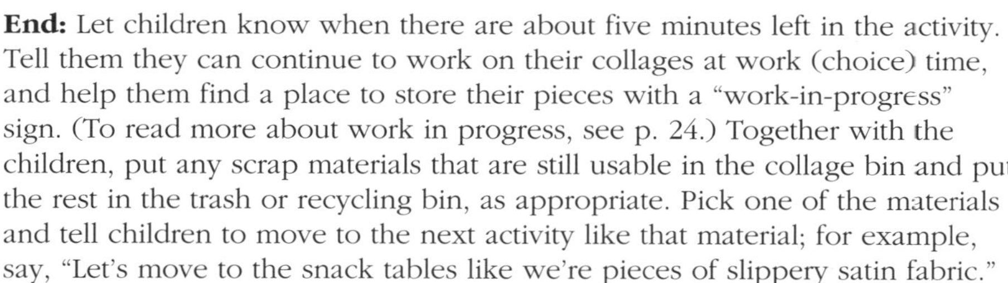

Scaffolding Learning at Each Developmental Level

Earlier	Middle	Later
Children may	**Children may**	**Children may**
Explore the sensory properties of the materials; for example, may crumple the paper, roll dried play dough bits between fingers, or squeeze glue over their paper.	Say something about the materials they are using, such as "This material is shiny."	Use the collage materials to make something representational, such as a human figure or an animal.
Adults can	**Adults can**	**Adults can**
Copy children's actions and describe what adults are doing: "I like to squeeze the glue and watch it spread out over the paper." Extend learning by asking children to describe the materials they are using and what they are doing, so adults can imitate them.	Acknowledge children's observations with a comment: "Yes, this fabric is shiny." Gently extend learning by encouraging children to find other materials that are the same or different: "I wonder what else you can find that looks shiny."	Talk about the details children have included in their work. Gently extend learning by wondering what other details children might include: point at a child's picture and say, "I see you used buttons to make the eyes — I wonder what materials you could use to make other parts of the face."

End: Let children know when there are about five minutes left in the activity. Tell them they can continue to work on their collages at work (choice) time, and help them find a place to store their pieces with a "work-in-progress" sign. (To read more about work in progress, see p. 24.) Together with the children, put any scrap materials that are still usable in the collage bin and put the rest in the trash or recycling bin, as appropriate. Pick one of the materials and tell children to move to the next activity like that material; for example, say, "Let's move to the snack tables like we're pieces of slippery satin fabric."

Follow-up: Ask children what other materials the class could add to the collage bin. At cleanup time each day, remind children to make use of the collage bin before they discard or recycle things.

2   *Lots of Lines*

> **Summary description:** After reading the book *Harold and the Purple Crayon,* children explore drawing different kinds of lines.

Time of day: Small-group time

Materials:

- *Harold and the Purple Crayon,* by Crockett Johnson
- Drawing materials (crayons, markers, colored pencils)
- Paper

Curriculum content: KDI 40. Art.
Also: KDI 26. Reading

COR Advantage item: X. Art.
Also: item P. Reading

Beginning: Read the storybook *Harold and the Purple Crayon.* (It helps if children are already familiar with the story so they can focus on the artwork as well as the narrative.) Chat with the children about all the things that Harold drew and how he used different types of lines to draw them. Distribute the drawing materials and say "I wonder what kinds of lines you will draw."

Middle: Circulate among the children and converse about the kinds of lines they are making. Use familiar words such as *thick, thin, long,* and *short,* and introduce new words such as *straight, squiggly, broken, connected, dash,* and *dot.* Describe what children are doing, and encourage children to describe their own actions when making the marks. Encourage them to try different drawing tools (for example, thin pencils versus thick markers) and to vary the amount of pressure they use. Encourage them to share their discoveries with one another.

The chart at right offers an example, at each developmental level, of what children may say and do, along with ideas for scaffolding (supporting and gently extending) children's learning at each level. For additional ideas, refer to the scaffolding chart for Art on page 32. To read more about scaffolding, see page 20.

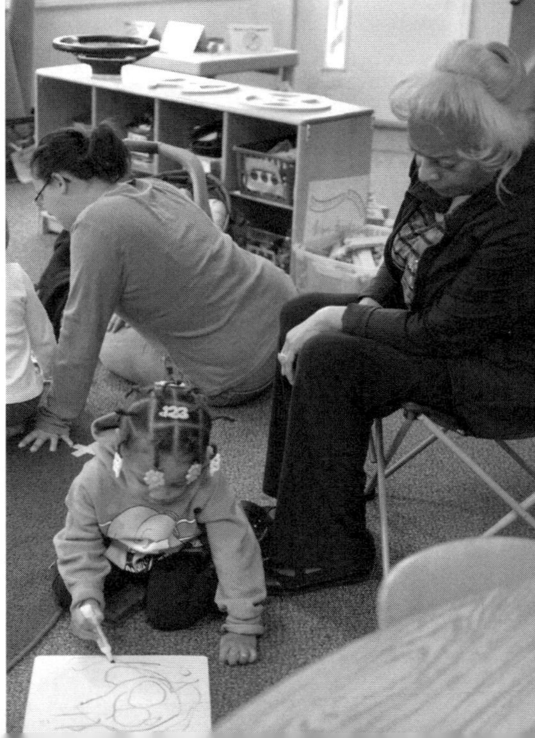

<table>
<tr><td colspan="3">Scaffolding Learning at Each Developmental Level</td></tr>
<tr><td>Earlier</td><td>Middle</td><td>Later</td></tr>
<tr>
<td>Children may

Look at the book rather than draw their own lines.</td>
<td>Children may

Explore one or two drawing materials, using them to make a couple of types of lines (e.g., thick and thin lines).</td>
<td>Children may

Explore many types of drawing materials and/or try to draw many types of lines with each material.</td>
</tr>
<tr>
<td>Adults can

Look at the book with children and talk about the lines and images Harold drew.

Extend learning by asking what other adventures Harold might have and how he could draw those.</td>
<td>Adults can

Ask children to describe what they did so adults can make the same type(s) of lines.

Extend learning by encouraging children to try different drawing materials and comparing the types of lines they can create with each.</td>
<td>Adults can

Ask children to describe the lines and what they did differently to create each one; for example, "How did you make this line straight but that one jagged?"

Extend learning by posing challenges — saying something like "I wonder what you could use to make a line that is wider than this one?"</td>
</tr>
</table>

End: Let children know that the activity will come to an end in five minutes. Together, put away the book and drawing materials. Tell the children to pretend they are drawing a line on the floor — like Harold did — as they move to the next activity in the daily routine.

Follow-up: Instead of reading a book, tell a story and ask children to draw their own kinds of lines to illustrate it. Encourage children to draw their own illustrations to familiar books.

3   *Wood Scrap Sculptures*

Summary description: Children build "sculptures" on a base or pedestal using scrap wood.

Time of day: Small-group time

Materials:

- Wood scraps of different shapes and sizes collected from lumberyards, home improvement stores, and parent contributions, with any rough edges sanded and any protruding nails or screws removed.
- Sturdy bases (for example, heavy cardboard or plywood), approximately one-foot square
- Fasteners such as glue, glue sticks, or tape
- Damp sponges or paper towels to wipe up spills

Curriculum content: KDI 40. Art. *Also:* KDI 17. Fine-motor skills and KDI 35. Spatial awareness

COR Advantage item: X. Art. *Also:* item J. Fine-motor skills and item T. Geometry, shapes, and spatial awareness

Beginning: Say something like "When artists build things with wood, they are called sculptures. I wonder what sculptures you can build." Give each child a base, a basket of wood scraps, and a glue stick.

Middle: Circulate and converse with children about the shapes and sizes of wood scraps they use in their sculptures. Use position words (such as *on top of* and *next to*) to describe how they arrange materials. Help them solve problems; for example, how to get something to stand up or how to attach pieces of wood to each other or to the base. Put the rest of the wood scraps and an assortment of fasteners in the middle of the table for the group to share.

The chart at right offers an example, at each developmental level, of what you may observe children say and do, along with ideas for scaffolding (supporting and gently extending) their learning at each developmental level. For additional ideas, refer to the scaffolding chart for Art on page 32. To read more about scaffolding, see page 20.

Scaffolding Learning at Each Developmental Level

Earlier	Middle	Later
Children may	***Children may***	***Children may***
Attach all the scraps directly to the base.	Stack two or three pieces to make a simple sculpture and say what it represents.	Construct a complex sculpture with many pieces of wood and position the wood to create a specific shape or representation.
Adults can	***Adults can***	***Adults can***
Select similar scraps and imitate childrens' actions. Extend learning by commenting on the sizes and shapes of the scraps, and the children's actions with the materials; encourage children to describe the materials and what they do with them.	Comment on how children stacked their wood pieces using spatial words: "You glued this long piece underneath the short piece." Extend learning by wondering out loud what would happen if children attached a piece "on top of" another piece or tried to make a "taller" sculpture, remembering to respect children's choices of how to use the materials.	Comment on the variety of shapes and sizes children use. Extend learning by asking children to describe the wood scraps and explain how they solved problems getting the materials to do what they wanted; encourage children to use less common position words such as *beneath*, *alongside*, and *protruding*; comment on how children choose particular pieces of wood because of their similarities to the objects they want to represent.

End: Give children a five-minute warning before the end of the activity. Clean up together, saving any usable wood scraps and letting children know where they can find them if they want to make more sculptures at work (choice) time. Help children store unfinished projects with a "work-in-progress" sign if they want to continue working on them. Suggest that children move "like a stick of wood" to the next activity in the daily routine.

Follow-up: Provide books and postcard reproductions of sculptures made of wood and other materials (stone, clay, metal, fabric) for children to look at. Take a field trip to a nearby park or other location (e.g., a public art site or a monument) where children can see sculptures in the community.

4   *Animal Creations*

> **Summary description:** After a field trip to see animals they are unlikely to encounter in their daily lives, children draw animals using their memories and their imagination.

Time of day: Small-group time, preceded by a field trip

Materials:
- Drawing supplies such as markers, crayons, or colored pencils
- Paper
- Photos of the field trip

Curriculum content: KDI 40. Art.
Also: KDI 51. Natural and physical world

COR Advantage item: X. Art.
Also: item DD. Natural and physical world

Beginning: Go on a field trip to a place where children can see animals they don't ordinarily encounter — for example, a pet store, petting farm, zoo, aquarium, or nature preserve. Take photos of the animals and their surroundings. The next day, spread out the photos and talk with the children about the field trip. Ask what they remember about how the animals looked (especially any distinguishing features), what habitat they lived in, what they ate, how they moved, the sounds they made, whether they played with each other, and so on. Then say something like "Today we're going to draw pictures of animals. I wonder what animals you will draw." Hand out paper and drawing materials.

Middle: Circulate among the children, conversing about their drawings, recollections of the field trip, or experiences with pets at home or neighborhood wildlife. Refer them to the photos so they can add more detail to their drawings. Don't expect them to make accurate representations or even to draw the animals they saw. Let them use their imagination and create their own animals.

The chart at right offers an example, at each developmental level, of what children may say and do, along with ideas for scaffolding (supporting and gently extending) children's learning at each level. For additional ideas, refer to the scaffolding chart for Art on page 32. To read more about scaffolding, see page 20.

Scaffolding Learning at Each Developmental Level

Earlier	Middle	Later
Children may	**Children may**	**Children may**
Draw things other than animals, or use the art materials to make non-representational drawings.	Draw their own pets or the animals they see in their neighborhood (e.g., squirrels, birds).	Draw animals they saw on the field trip or invent their own, and may include several details.
Adults can	**Adults can**	**Adults can**
Converse about the qualities of the materials children are using and the visual effects they make: "You're drawing swirls all over your paper." Extend learning by asking children what they remember about the field trip, especially anything visual that stuck with them; for example, about the animals, the setting, the bus trip, and so on.	Talk with children about the characteristics they are representing, such as the animals' color(s), distinctive markings (e.g., adults might use the words *stripes, plumage,* or *scales* in their comments), and other features. Extend learning by encouraging children to add other details to their animal drawings.	Encourage children to label and describe the details in their drawings. Extend learning by helping children recall and represent details beyond the animal itself, such as where it lives (cave, nest, tree limb), its habitat (sea, woods, jungle, ice floe), the food it eats, the climate (warm or cold weather), the rest of its "family" or litter, and so on.

End: Alert children when small-group time is five minutes from ending. Put away the materials together. Encourage children to take their drawings home or, if they want, to display them in the classroom. Have children move to the next activity in the daily routine like an animal they saw on the field trip.

Follow-up: Add information books and storybooks to the classroom, including books with pictures (photographs as well as illustrations) of animals in their natural habitat. Post photos of the field trip where parents and children can talk about the experience at dropoff and pickup times. If your program has a secure website or newsletter, share the photos with families.

5

Aluminum Foil Sculptures

Summary description: Children explore the sculptural possibilities of working with aluminum foil.

Time of day: Small-group time

Materials:

♦ Aluminum foil (two sheets to start with; extra sheets as needed)

♦ Wrapping or decorating materials, such as ribbon and pipe cleaners

Curriculum content: KDI 40. Art. *Also:* KDI 35. Spatial awareness

COR Advantage item: X. Art. *Also:* item T. Geometry: Shapes and spatial awareness

Beginning: Talk about things you've seen the children fold, roll, or crumple — for example, paper towels, napkins, or leaves. Say something like "Aluminum foil is another material you can roll, fold, or crumple into different shapes." Demonstrate. Continue by saying something like "When artists do that, they call it making a sculpture. I wonder what sculptures you will make." Give each child one or two pieces of aluminum foil.

Middle: Circulate among the children. Talk about the how the foil looks and feels, how children's actions affect the foil's appearance, and what, if anything, they make with the foil. Add words related to texture (*smooth*, *bumpy*, *pointy*), action (*bend*, *twist*), and shape (*curved*, *straight*, *round*, *flat*) to help children experience their art from various sensory perspectives. Encourage children to use the supplementary materials, if desired, to wrap or decorate their sculptures.

The chart at right offers an example, at each developmental level, of what children may say and do, along with ideas for scaffolding (supporting and gently extending) their learning at each level. For additional ideas, refer to the scaffolding chart for Art on page 32. To read more about scaffolding, see page 20.

Scaffolding Learning at Each Developmental Level

Earlier	Middle	Later
Children may	***Children may***	***Children may***
Explore the foil without trying to make something.	Accidentally make something and then label it; for example, they may crumple the foil and then say, "Hey — I made a ball!"	Intentionally make something — for example, they may say they are going to make a dog and mold the foil so it has ears and a tail.
Adults can	***Adults can***	***Adults can***
Describe children's actions; for example, "You flattened it" or "You scrunched the foil." Extend learning by encouraging children to handle the foil in different ways and commenting on how they are transforming the material: "It was shiny and smooth — now it's rough and wrinkled."	Acknowledge children's observations by saying something like "You squeezed the foil between your hands and made it round, like a ball." Extend learning by asking children what they think would happen if they used their hands in a different way with the foil.	Comment on the representational features children have included and ask them to describe how they made them. Extend learning by wondering what else children could make with the foil and what they would have to do to make it; for example, if the child suggests a giraffe, adults might ask the child how he or she would make its long neck.

End: Give children a three- to five-minute warning before the end of the activity time, and then put away the materials together. Let the children know where the foil will be stored if they want to use it again at work (choice) time. Tell them to "scrunch" a part of their body as they move to the next activity in the daily routine.

Follow-up: Supply other materials the children can mold. For example, in addition to play dough and clay, offer beeswax, wet sand, and newspaper. Provide photographs, exhibition posters, and reproduction postcards of sculptures made of metal and other materials.

6 *Mirror, Mirror*

Summary description: Children look at themselves in a mirror and draw self-portraits. They may also choose to draw someone else at their table. Looking in the mirror or closely observing another person encourages them to include more details.

Time of day: Small-group time

Materials:
- Small (handheld) plastic mirror
- Drawing materials, such as crayons or colored pencils (*note:* the finer the point on the drawing tool, the more it encourages and enables children to include details)
- Drawing paper

Curriculum content: KDI 40. Art. *Also:* KDI 17. Fine-motor skills and KDI 53. Diversity

COR Advantage item: X. Art. *Also:* item J. Fine-motor skills and item FF. Knowledge of self and others

Beginning: Say something like "Artists draw and paint pictures of many things. Some artists like to make pictures of people. If I were going to draw a picture of myself, I could look in a mirror to see what I look like." To model the process, look at yourself in a mirror and describe what you see; for example, you might say, "I have curly hair and brown eyes, and I wear glasses." Draw that on your paper. Give each child a mirror and drawing materials and say, "What do you see when you look at yourself in the mirror? I wonder how you will draw that."

Middle: Circulate among the children and converse with them about what they see in the mirror and what they are drawing. Talk about the similarities and differences in the children's physical characteristics, being factual and taking care not to make judgments. If children are interested, they can also draw someone else at the table. Encourage them to observe the other person both before and as they draw. Occasionally offer a prompt, such as "What else do you see?"

The chart at right offers an example, at each developmental level, of what children may say and do, along with ideas for scaffolding (supporting and gently extending) children's learning at each level. For additional ideas, refer to the scaffolding chart for Art on page 32. To read more about scaffolding, see page 20.

Scaffolding Learning at Each Developmental Level

Earlier	Middle	Later
Children may	**Children may**	**Children may**
Be more interested in looking in the mirror than in drawing themselves.	Draw a simple representation with one or two facial features.	Include several facial features in their drawings.
Adults can	**Adults can**	**Adults can**
Talk about what children see when they look at their reflection; describe, and encourage children to describe, children's features.	Label and describe what children have drawn, commenting on artistic features such as line, shape, or color selection; focus on the process, not the product, and the choices children make while creating their drawings.	Encourage children to talk about each detail and how they went about drawing it.
Extend learning by encouraging children to look at an adult's face (or reflection) and discuss how the adult's features are similar to and/or different from theirs.	Extend the learning by wondering what other features children could add; encourage them to keep looking in the mirror for more ideas.	Extend learning by suggesting children observe another person and draw him or her, including as many details as possible; put the two pictures side by side and discuss their similarities and differences.

End: Give children a three- to five-minute warning before the end of the activity time. (Because there are no "messy" materials to clean up, it can be on the shorter side.) Together with the children, put the materials away. Tell children where they can find the mirrors if they want to use them at work time. To transition, play "I Spy" by describing a feature of each child, in turn, who should go to the next activity ("I spy someone with red, curly hair. Yes — David! David may go to the snack table").

Follow-up: Have children bring in photos of themselves or family members and use these as references for making drawings. Provide information books with photos or detailed illustrations of the kinds of things children in your class like to draw (such as plants, animals, buildings, vehicles, construction equipment). Encourage children to refer to the books and add details to their own drawings.

7 Painting With Irregular Objects

Summary description: Children paint with household and natural objects not ordinarily used for painting.

Time of day: Small-group time

Materials:

- Paint (one or two colors so children focus on using the materials, not on mixing paints)
- Paper
- Household and natural objects children don't associate with painting; for example, feathers, crumpled newspaper, corks, golf balls, whisks, sponges, suction cups, twigs, sea shells, rocks
- Damp sponges and paper towels for wiping up (spread newspaper on the table for easier cleanup)

Curriculum content: KDI 40. Art.
Also: KDI 5. Use of resources and KDI 17. Fine-motor skills

COR Advantage item: X. Art.
Also: item B. Problem solving with materials and item J. Fine-motor skills

Beginning: Talk with the children about how they usually paint with brushes. Say something like "Today we're going to paint with different tools." Show them and label (name) the variety of objects. Give each child paper and a couple of tools to get started. Leave the other tools on the table for them to share.

Middle: Try various tools yourself. Walk around the table and talk with children about the tools they are using and the effects each has — for example, the types of marks it makes, the texture it leaves on the page, whether it holds a lot of paint or only a little.

The chart at right offers an example, at each developmental level, of what children may say and do, along with ideas for scaffolding (supporting and gently extending) their learning at each level. For additional ideas, refer to the scaffolding chart for Art on page 32. To read more about scaffolding, see page 20.

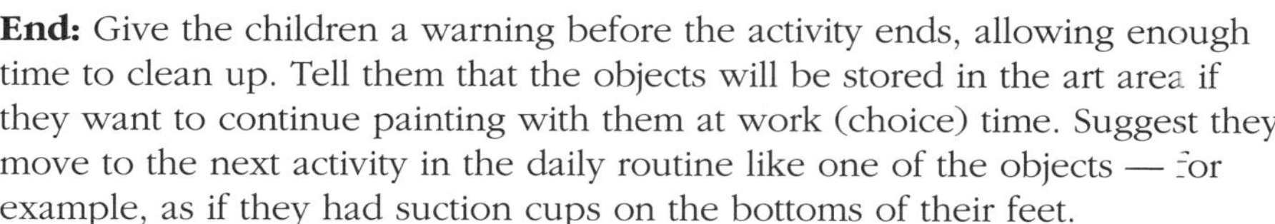

Scaffolding Learning at Each Developmental Level

Earlier	Middle	Later
Children may	**Children may**	**Children may**
Explore the objects without using them to paint.	Use the objects to paint with and to see what kinds of effects they make.	Use objects to make specific designs or representations.
Adults can	**Adults can**	**Adults can**
Explore the objects alongside children and imitate their actions. Extend learning by labeling and describing the aesthetic properties of the objects children choose: "This sea shell is striped with many different colors. I wonder if anything else here has lots of colors."	Comment on the artistic effects children create: "The twig made a skinny line, but the sponge made a wide line." Extend learning by encouraging children to anticipate what effects various objects will have: "I wonder what kind of mark the whisk will leave on the paper."	Acknowledge what children say they have done or made: "Yes, I see that you used a feather to paint branches on a tree." Extend learning by asking what other tools children could use to add further details to their paintings: "Suppose you wanted to make more flowers — what other tool could you use? How does it look the same as (or different from) when you used the cork?"

End: Give the children a warning before the activity ends, allowing enough time to clean up. Tell them that the objects will be stored in the art area if they want to continue painting with them at work (choice) time. Suggest they move to the next activity in the daily routine like one of the objects — for example, as if they had suction cups on the bottoms of their feet.

Follow-up: Provide other objects to paint with in the art area. Ask families to donate old kitchen utensils or carpentry tools. Point out interesting textural effects in the classroom furnishings (such as feathered patterns on fabric) or on neighborhood walks (such as paint rolled on stucco).

8

How Does Your Garden Grow?

Summary description: After a walking field trip to look at neighborhood gardens, children make their own classroom garden using natural materials.

Time of day: Small-group time (preceded by a field trip)

Materials:

♦ Natural materials such as twigs, leaves, dried flower petals and stalks, small- and medium-sized stones, pebbles, bark, acorns, pine cones, reeds, seed pods, clumps of moss

♦ Large sheet of brown paper (the "soil") spread on the floor or table top

Curriculum content: KDI 40. Art. *Also:* KDI 45. Observing and KDI 51. Natural and physical world

COR Advantage item: X. Art. *Also:* item BB. Observing and classifying and item DD. Natural and physical world

Beginning: Take a neighborhood walk to see what is growing in gardens, yards, parks, median strips, planters, and window boxes. Try to observe a variety of flowers, vegetables, trees, shrubs, and ground covers. The next day, tell children that they are going to make their own garden. (If your program already has an outdoor garden, and children comment on this, say something like, "We're going to also make a pretend garden right here in the classroom.") Show children the "soil" and the materials and say, "I wonder what we'll plant in our garden." Give each child a basket of materials and leave the rest in the middle of the table (or on the floor) for them to share.

Middle: Kneel beside children as they create their garden. Encourage them to name and describe the materials and what they do with them and, if they are interested, to name the plants and imagine their smell (flowers) or taste (vegetables). Wonder aloud how big the plants will grow as the children arrange and space them on the soil. Comment that creating a garden is like making a painting or a collage in the earth.

The chart at right offers an example, at different developmental levels, of what children may say and do, along with ideas for scaffolding (supporting and gently extending) their learning at each level. For additional ideas, refer to the scaffolding chart for Art on page 32. To read more about scaffolding, see page 20.

End: Give children a five-minute

Scaffolding Learning at Each Developmental Level

Earlier	Middle	Later
Children may	***Children may***	***Children may***
Explore the properties of the materials or use them to make things other than plants.	Include one or two characteristics of plants in their work.	Include many features of the plants and gardens they saw on the walk.
Adults can	***Adults can***	***Adults can***
Work alongside children and copy their actions. Extend learning by asking children to describe what they are doing so the adults can try to do the same thing: "Show (or tell) me what you did with the leaves to make them crumble."	Comment on the parts of a plant they represent: "You used the twig for a stem and put a flower (or tomato) on top." Extend learning by wondering what additional details children might include and by talking about other plant and garden features they saw on the walk (using vocabulary like *leaves, tendrils*, and *mulch*) and what materials children could use to make those.	Discuss the characteristics of the materials children choose that make them appropriate for representing particular features: "This straw is thin like the tendrils on the vine." Extend learning by talking about the overall artistic effects of composing the garden, such as contrasts in color or texture, or how some areas are crowded while others are spread out.

warning before the end of the activity time, and then put away the unused materials together. Remind children of where the materials will be stored if they want to continue using them at choice (work) time. Take a photo of the garden to share with families. Have children pretend to be a plant that grows bigger and bigger as they move to the next activity in the daily routine.

Follow-up: Provide books with pictures of gardens, such as seed catalogs, home and garden magazines, and landscaping books. Bring in reproductions of famous artwork featuring gardens such as Monet's water lilies or pieced quilts with flower designs. If you plant an outdoor garden with the children, talk about its aesthetic properties as the flowers and vegetables start to grow.

9

Tread on Me (Making Imprints)

Summary description: Children make imprints in moldable materials using non-art tools that create a variety of lines and textures.

Time of day: Small-group time

Materials:

♦ A large ball or lump of moldable material such as clay, play dough, or softened beeswax

♦ Objects such as cooking utensils, carpentry tools, and clothing accessories that make imprints; for example, a pastry wheel, cookie cutters, a garlic press, a butter mold, a hand drill, wide-gauge mesh, costume jewelry, a mallet, picture hooks, wing nuts, electrical outlet guards, buttons, rubber soles

♦ Base that is approximately one-foot square and made of sturdy cardboard, plywood, or plastic

Curriculum content: KDI 40. Art. *Also:* KDI 45. Observing and KDI 46. Classifying

COR Advantage item: X. Art. *Also:* item BB. Observing and classifying

Beginning: Show photos and talk about things the children have seen that make imprints or impressions, such as tire treads, cookie cutters, and footprints. Say that artists sometimes make pictures or designs by pressing objects into soft materials, such as clay, to create what is called an "imprint." Demonstrate with one of the tools, and talk with children about its effects. Explain that today they will be making imprints with different tools. Give each child a base, a ball of moldable material, and two tools. Leave additional tools in the middle of the table for children to share.

Middle: Circulate among the children, and converse with them about the effects created by the tools they use. Encourage them to explore a wide range of objects and to look at one another's work. Introduce vocabulary words to label the tools and describe the lines and textures they leave — for example, *butter mold, screwdriver handle, wavy, checkered.*

The chart at right offers an example, at each developmental level, of what children may say and do, along with ideas for scaffolding (supporting and gently extending) the children's learning. For additional ideas, refer to the scaffolding chart for Art on page 32. To read more about scaffolding, see page 20.

Scaffolding Learning at Each Developmental Level

Earlier	Middle	Later
Children may	**Children may**	**Children may**
Press their hands and fingers into the material.	Systematically explore and compare the effects of different tools.	Use the tools to create representational images or designs.
Adults can	**Adults can**	**Adults can**
Imitate and describe children's actions. Extend learning by choosing a tool and trying it themselves; invite children to try the tool too (while respecting the choice of any who decide not to); converse with children about the marks made with the tool — for example, "The screwdriver makes a thin, squiggly line," "The drill makes a deep imprint," or "The butter mold leaves a pattern in the clay."	Validate children's observations and comparisons — saying, for example, "Yes, the bottom of the sneaker made little squares in the clay" or "I see how the chisel handle leaves a wider mark than the paintbrush handle." Extend learning by asking children to anticipate what the effect of a particular tool might be: "What kind of mark do you suppose this button will make?"	Create the same effects with the materials; describe what children are doing and making, and encourage the children themselves to describe what they are doing, while repeating children's words and adding new ones (e.g., *checkerboard*). Extend learning by encouraging children to add more details and to try other tools: "What else could you add to your house? I wonder which tool you will use to create it."

End: Warn the children five minutes before the activity ends, and then put things away together. Let children know that the materials will be available for use in the art area, and help children who want to continue working on their imprints to carry them to a safe place with a work-in-progress sign. Tell the children to pretend they are leaving imprints in the mud (or snow) as they move to the next activity in the daily routine.

Follow-up: Bring tools outside for children to use for making imprints in sand piles. As a group, look at the children's footprints and hand prints in mud or snow, and be on the lookout for imprints by people and vehicles on neighborhood walks. Ask families to bring in objects the children can use to make imprints, such as old athletic shoes, carved buttons from used clothing, and costume jewelry.

10   *Outdoor Weaving*

> **Summary description:** Children use structures in the outdoor play area, such as a fence, to weave a variety of materials in and out.

Time of day: Small-group time, held outside

Materials:

♦ Structure that can serve as a "loom" such as a chain-link or wooden-slat fence, stair railings, climber or slide ladder
♦ Things to weave with, such as yarn, ribbon, string, pipe cleaners, bendable twigs and stems, feathers, paper and cardboard strips

Curriculum content: KDI 40. Art. *Also:* KDI 35. Spatial awareness and KDI 38. Patterns

COR Advantage item: X. Art. *Also:* item T. Geometry: Shapes and spatial awareness and item V. Patterns

Beginning: Show the children photos of rugs, blankets, wall hangings, and other woven objects and talk with them about the art and process of weaving. Explain that a weaving is often made on a "loom" and that artists weave yarn and other things in and out of the openings (show a picture of a weaving in progress). Say to children that today they will use a fence (or other structure) as a loom and weave things between the spaces. Make sure each child has an area in which to work, and then hand out two materials for them to start with. Keep additional materials in easy reach for them to explore.

Middle: Move among the children as they work. Comment on their choice of materials and how they use them. Introduce position and direction words such as *over and under, behind, between, in back (in front) of,* and so on. Help children solve problems — for example, if a material is too short to weave in and out as many times as they want, or if they are having trouble bending it.

The chart at right offers an example, at each developmental level, of what children may say and do, along with ideas for scaffolding (supporting and gently extending) learning at each level. For additional ideas, refer to the scaffolding chart for Art on page 32. For more about scaffolding, see page 20.

Scaffolding Learning at Each Developmental Level

Earlier	Middle	Later
Children may	***Children may***	***Children may***
Explore the materials without trying to weave them through the structure.	Comment on how easy or hard it is to weave with different materials and/or the different visual effects each creates.	Create patterns — for example, alternating rows of two colors or two types of materials.
Adults can	***Adults can***	***Adults can***
Explore the materials alongside children, commenting on properties such as color, texture, and flexibility.	Use the materials and repeat children's observations: "My twig broke the first time too but the ribbon was easy to weave in and out."	Refer specifically to what children have made as a pattern.
Extend learning by weaving with one of the materials, discussing such actions with the children and encouraging them to try weaving (while respecting their choice if they decide not to).	Extend learning by asking children why they think materials are more or less flexible or have certain effects: "I wonder why the stem is easier to bend than the twig"; encourage children to find solutions to the problems they encounter.	Extend learning by encouraging children to describe the elements in their pattern, and by encouraging children to find and describe other patterns (e.g., in the clothing they and others are wearing, in the brickwork or plants in the outdoor play area, and in the other surrounding structures).

End: Give children a warning signal that the activity time will be ending. If possible, leave the weaving outside for families to see at pickup time or (if it is not safe or feasible) take photos. Spread out the baskets of materials in a line between the fence (or weaving area) and the door, and ask the children to weave their bodies in and out of the baskets as they move inside. Ask the last "weavers" to help carry the baskets back to the classroom.

Follow-up: Put the materials in baskets for the children to carry outdoors at outside time. Provide books and reproduction postcards of various types of weaving. Encourage families to contribute materials the children can use for weaving. Make frame looms out of canvas stretchers (available at art supply and frame shops) for children to weave inside the classroom. (*Note:* Make the looms a foot square or smaller; tack a row of nails on the top and bottom, and string columns of sturdy twine between the nails. Children can then weave materials over and under the twine.)

Activities for

Music

Vincenzio [Galileo's father] taught Galileo to sing, and to play the organ and other instruments. In the course of this instruction, he introduced the boy to the Pythagorean rule of musical ratios, which required strict obedience in tuning and composition to the numerical properties of notes in a scale ... When Vincenzio filled a room with weighted strings of varying lengths, diameters, and tensions to test certain harmonic ideas, Galileo joined him as his assistant. It seems safe to say that Galileo, who gets credit for being the father of experimental physics, may have learned the rudiments and value of experimentation from his own father's efforts. (Sobel, 2001, pp. 16 & 18)

The Development of Music in Children

Young children and music are natural partners. Babies are soothed by lullabies or wriggle with pleasure when they hear a livelier tune. Toddlers repeat familiar song fragments and gestures. Preschoolers can differentiate musical styles, learn the words and melodies to songs or make up their own, and play simple instruments. Like the other areas

of the creative arts, music is a language that young children can use to communicate their thoughts and feelings. Researchers have identified four areas in which musical development proceeds in young children.

Developing rhythmic knowledge. Perceiving the "time" elements of sound is fundamental to understanding and creating music. While this ability begins in toddlerhood, a sense of rhythmic structure is much better established in preschool (Stellaccio & McCarthy, 1999). Repeated experiences with music that has a prominent beat is key to this development (Weikart, 2000).

Developing tonal knowledge. Infants as young as three months try to match the pitch of their voice to the sounds they hear. Toddlers can reproduce melodic intervals (sing a note and the one that is a step higher or lower). By age three, children can sing with a lyrical quality, and by age five, they can match tones with accuracy (Bayless & Ramsey, 2004). This ability, called "tonal competence," is highly dependent on their early experiences, which must include physical activity. For example, young children who sing and move their bodies high or low to match their singing voice have greater pitch awareness than those who just listen to the music (Scott-Kasner, 1992).

Understanding the emotional elements in music. Because music has many emotional qualities, listening and responding to it is a form of social interaction. Although the research is limited, it appears that preschoolers can identify the feelings conveyed by music and respond appropriately (Kemple, Batey, & Hartle, 2005). For example, they speed up or enlarge their motions when they hear lively music, and reduce the rate or size of their gestures when the music is quiet. Repeated experiences with interactive musical games also appears to increase empathy in young children (Rabinowich, Cross, & Burnard, 2013), further evidence of its social and emotional pull.

Musical creativity and play. Young children are quite inventive when they chant, sing, and use instruments during free play. For example, they inflect their voices to depict animals (barking) or machines (humming), and make up or vary familiar songs to accompany rhythmic actions such as hammering or rocking a doll. Not surprisingly, children in open-ended play settings engage in more spontaneous musical behaviors than those in highly adult-directed programs (Greata, 2006).

Emerging brain research also highlights the relationship between music and neural development, with implications for literacy and mathematics. For example, children pay more attention when verbal instructions are accompanied by a steady beat, since beat is processed in the same area of the brain that controls attention (Geist, Geist, & Kuznok, 2012). A growing body of evidence finds that music training enhances spatial reasoning and computational skills (Scripp, 2002), the ability to segment speech sounds (Francois, Chobert, Besson, & Schon, 2013), and fluency in reading (Kim & Robinson, 2010). In sum, music can be a valuable part of the early childhood curriculum, both for the inherent pleasure it brings and also as a tool to enhance other learning.

Materials and Equipment That Support Music

Although children today often hear sounds and music on electronic devices, it is critical for them to experience the noises, melodies, and rhythms that come directly from the objects and actions that produce them. Provide children with the types of equipment and materials listed here to encourage their musical experiments and discoveries:

- Sound-making objects (timers, metronome, mechanical toys — items that beep, whirr, or clang)

- Simple percussion instruments (drums, tambourines, bells, xylophone, triangle, maracas, shakers and bean bags filled with different materials, rhythm sticks, cymbals, trash can lids, metal or plastic plates, thumb piano or keyboard, slatted fence)

- Simple woodwind instruments (whistle, harmonica, kazoo, recorder, horns, party favors, chimes)

- Simple string instruments (child-size ukulele or guitar, marimba, zither, dulcimer)

- Song books

- Music players

For additional ideas, see *The HighScope Preschool Curriculum* (Epstein & Hohmann, 2012, Chapter 6, pp. 171–221).

Teaching Strategies That Support Music

Teachers can use the following strategies every day to help young children develop their musical knowledge and skills:

Look for opportunities to listen to, identify, and create sounds with children.

Preschoolers enjoy representing objects and events with sounds — a barking dog, a ticking clock, a blaring siren. Encourage them to use their voices and bodies to create sounds, and provide a variety of noise-making materials. Create opportunities to listen by going outside in nature or by playing sound guessing games. Label and describe different sounds, and encourage children to do the same.

Sing with children.

Children love to sing and to hear others sing, so sing with them every day. Introduce a variety of songs from different musical genres, including those from other countries and cultures that families listen to at home. Invite parents to sing with you, and use song sheets, secure web pages, and other modes for sharing the songs children learn at school so they can sing them at home. Sing throughout the day; for example, as the children transition from one activity to another.

Play a wide variety of recorded and live music.

Play different types of instrumental and vocal music, such as folk, jazz, and classical; also play different rhythms, such as marches, waltzes, and tangos. Play primarily instrumental selections; the brain pays attention to language first and may miss the musical elements if it is focusing on words. Live music is a special treat for children and adults alike. Invite staff, parents, and guests to play music or teach simple songs while children sing, clap, move, or accompany them on simple instruments. Use music to facilitate transitions — for example, to speed along cleanup time. However, do not play background music while children are engaged in other work or group activities. The noise is distracting and makes listening and conversation difficult.

Provide simple instruments.

Preschoolers especially enjoy playing instruments that involve hand and body movements (see above list). Provide instruments that allow children to use both hands (such as triangles or hand drums) or to hold one in each hand (such as rhythm sticks or maracas). Be sure the instruments available in the classroom represent the children's cultures. Encourage children to play instruments during work (choice) time, make plans to include them at small-group times (for children to explore their sounds) and large-group times (as cues for starting and stopping), use them to signal transitions, and bring them outside. Instruments can also be used to represent characters or actions when you read books or act out stories with the children.

For more information on teaching strategies that support music in preschool, see Epstein (2012, Chapter 4.)

Incorporating Cultural Diversity in Music

"Music is a non-verbal form of communication and can bridge the cultural divides between people of different backgrounds" (Pica, 2009, p. 74). Of all the art forms, music may be the one whose diversity is most accessible to the public, especially via downloads of world music on the Internet. Use a variety of search terms to explore different artists, genres, instruments, and techniques. If possible, let the children see (and touch) the instruments and other objects creating the sounds they hear. If these are not readily available, provide drawings and photos for children to look at as they listen. Here are some suggestions to get you started. Consult with children's families and local musicians (performers and composers) for other ideas.

Artists. You might talk about and provide samples of music by the following individual and group artists: Wyclef Jean (Haitian); Ladysmith Black Mambazo (South African); Shakira (Lebanese-Colombian); Ravi Shankar (Indian); Bob and Ziggy Marley (Jamaican); Clifton Chenier (Cajun and Creole); Django Reinhardt (Belgian Roma jazz musician); Amadou and Mariam (blind musicians from Mali); Manu Chao (Spanish); Ska Cubano (Jamaican and Cuban); Dobet Gnahoré (West African musician and dancer); Carolina Chocolate Drops (African-American).

Genres. The following are musical genres you could introduce children to, which together reflect a diversity of cultures and influences: Japanese koto; Indian raga; Tibetan chants; Eastern European polkas; Celtic harp; South African Mbaqanga; Tuvan throat singing; Native American flute music; zydeco; mariachi; samba; flamenco; tango; bluegrass; and nonwestern scales, rhythms, and inflections.

Materials (ethnic instruments). You could introduce children to the following instruments, which reflect the music of a variety of cultures: kora (West African harp); Indian sitar; Australian didgeridoo; Tibetan bowls; gamelan (Indonesian ensemble featuring gongs, drums, metallophone, flutes, and strings); tablas (Indian hand drum).

Adapting Music Materials and Activities for Children With Special Needs

Materials can be manipulated in many ways to produce musical sounds. Think flexibly as you adapt instruments and other noise-making materials for the children in your program to explore making music. Combine sounds with other sensory cues to help those with limited hearing. Take advantage of the fact that many children with impaired hearing can feel vibrations. Finally, be sensitive to the fact that children have different tolerances for the volume and range of musical sounds. Try the ideas below and adjust them, as needed, for the children in your program.

- Add pictures and visual cues when giving directions (for example, sign as well as sing songs).

- For children who have trouble grasping handheld instruments (such as bells), attach them with Velcro straps.

- For children who have difficulty with fine-motor coordination, substitute a door stop (or small wedged block) as a pick to strum instruments.

- Provide sound amplifiers.

- Offer headphones, foam headbands, or other ear covers to children who are sensitive to loud sounds.

Adapting Music Materials and Activities for Children Who Are Dual Language Learners (DLLs)

Instrumental music can be understood by young children, regardless of their English proficiency. Learning the words to simple songs is an effective technique for helping preschoolers practice their emerging English language skills, and it also provides an opportunity for children and families to introduce songs in their home languages to others in the class. The following suggestions will help DLL children use music to communicate with teachers and classmates.

- Encourage children to name and describe, in their home language, the songs they sing and the instruments they use, and provide the English equivalent.

- Label song books, music players, and instruments in the language(s) children in the classroom speak, as well as in English.

- Encourage DLL children and native English speakers to collaborate during music activities, sharing their discoveries and ideas, and helping one another solve problems.

- Sing and play songs in the language(s) children in the classroom speak. Invite family members to teach songs in their home language(s) to the class.

- Partner DLLs with native English speakers during music activities. Act as a translator to help them understand and carry out one another's ideas. Check with DLL children to make sure you have correctly understood and communicated their ideas. Check with native English speakers to make sure they understand the DLL children's intentions.

1 *Melodic Materials*

Summary description: Using random pitches, children sing descriptions of objects, tools, and other materials.

Time of day: Small-group time

Materials:
Objects, tools, and other items children frequently play with such as blocks of different shapes, sizes, and materials (Legos, wooden blocks, cardboard blocks); people and animal figures; construction tools (hammer, screwdriver, nuts and bolts, golf tees); art supplies (paintbrush, crayons, paper, yarn, ball of modeling clay); cooking and eating utensils (silverware, plates and cups, sauce pans, spatulas, wooden spoons); dress-up clothes (hats and helmets, scarves and belts, shoes, badges); and books (of different sizes and on various subjects, board books, soft cover books)

Curriculum content: KDI 41. Music. *Also:* KDI 45. Observing

COR Advantage item: Y. Music. *Also:* item BB. Observing and classifying

Beginning: Tell the children that today they are going to "sing" about the things they like to play and work with. Pick up an object and, using random pitches (that is, not a melody), sing "This is a paintbrush." Pick up another object and sing, "I pound nails with a hammer." Encourage the children to each pick an object; say to them, "I wonder what you will sing about the item you chose."

Middle: Listen to what the children sing. Encourage them to sing descriptions of the materials and/or what they do with them. Match their words and pitches, and occasionally introduce new ones. Comment on whether a pitch is higher or lower than the previous one. Invite children to choose a variety of materials and add a few more midway through the activity.

The chart at right offers an example, at each developmental level, of what children may say and do, along with ideas for scaffolding (supporting and gently extending) children's learning at each level. For additional ideas, refer to the scaffolding chart for Music on page 33. You can read more about scaffolding on page 20.

Scaffolding Learning at Each Developmental Level		
Earlier	**Middle**	**Later**
Children may	***Children may***	***Children may***
Name or describe an object or material without singing.	Sing a short phrase or sentence to describe an object or how they use a tool.	Sing full sentences or string phrases and sentences together.
Adults can	***Adults can***	***Adults can***
Acknowledge and repeat what childern say; for example, "You have a hammer."	Sing back children's pitches and words and comment on the range of pitches children use: "You sang *doll* with a high pitch and *bed* with a lower pitch."	Say something like "What other object can you sing about?" and encourage children to add details to their descriptions: "I wonder what else you can sing about the frying pan."
Extend learning by singing back children's words (using random pitches) — for example, "Paint with red paint."	Extend learning by turning children's phrases into sentences or by adding another sentence; for example, if a child sings, "A red Lego," an adult might sing, "You're holding a red Lego," and if a child sings, "I got a hammer," the adult can repeat and extend it to "You have a hammer — you use it to pound nails."	Extend learning by encouraging children to listen to and imitate one another's sung descriptions (pitches and words) and by asking children to figure out whether a pitch is higher or lower than, or the same as, another pitch.

End: Go around the table and have each child sing about one more material. Together with the children, put the materials away. Have the children sing their actions, still using random pitches, as they move to the next activity in the daily routine.

Follow-up: At work (choice) time, as you circulate around the classroom, now and then "sing" in random pitches about the materials the children are using and what they are doing with them. Encourage children to do the same. Announce transitions with random-pitch words — for example, you might sing, "Five minutes to cleanup time."

2 Sounds of Nature

> **Summary description:** Children explore the sounds and musical qualities of natural materials.

Time of day: Small-group time

Materials:

Natural materials that can be used separately or together to make a variety of sounds, such as rocks, pebbles, sticks, dried leaves, dried pods, tall dry grasses, wood chips, shells, acorns, tree bark, and so on (choose features native to your area and/or the season)

Curriculum content: KDI 41. Music. *Also:* KDI 51. Natural and physical world

COR Advantage item: Y. Music. *Also:* item DD. Natural and physical world

Beginning: Tell the children that natural materials can be used as "instruments" because they make interesting sounds. Demonstrate, for example, by crushing leaves between your hands or hitting a small stone on a larger rock. Talk with the children about the sound qualities they hear. Distribute the materials and say something like "I wonder how you will use the things in your baskets to make sounds like instruments."

Middle: Encourage children to experiment with a variety of natural materials. Say things like "I wonder what different sounds you can make with a stick" or "What do you see that might make a similar (or a different) sound?" Talk about how the sounds remind them of other musical sounds — for example, you might say, "The rustling grasses remind me of when we rubbed the whisk broom on the cymbals." Describe and encourage children to describe the sounds they both hear and create.

The chart at right offers an example, at each developmental level, of what children may say and do, along with ideas for scaffolding (supporting and gently extending) learning at each level. For additional ideas, refer to the scaffolding chart for Music on page 33. To read more about scaffolding, see page 20.

Scaffolding Learning at Each Developmental Level

Earlier	Middle	Later
Children may	***Children may***	***Children may***
Explore sound-making properties of one or two materials; for example, shoveling pebbles with their hands or crushing dried leaves.	Investigate multiple materials in different combinations; for example, using a stick to scrape bark, stir leaves, and tap on a rock.	Incorporate steady beat into their explorations.
Adults can	***Adults can***	***Adults can***
Imitate children's actions. Extend learning by referring children to the sounds other children are investigating: "Ilana is using pebbles too, dropping them on the big rock — let's listen."	Comment on the sounds children produce, using vocabulary words such as *rustle*, *swish*, *plink*, and *scrape*. Extend learning by encouraging children to explore more variations by altering the tempo or pitch of the sound (e.g., smaller stones produce a higher pitch than larger ones).	Use their materials to create the same beat and alter the beat to see if children imitate. Extend learning by inviting children to make up songs to accompany the sounds they create.

End: Give children a three-minute warning. Together with the children, gather the materials and tell the children where the materials will be stored if they want to continue experimenting with them at work (choice) time. Tell children to "move in a way that makes a sound" (for example, stomp or shuffle their feet) as they transition to the next activity in the daily routine.

Follow-up: Continue to look for natural sound-making objects outside, and bring them into the classroom for children to explore.

3 *Making and Shaking Maracas*

> **Summary description:** Children make maracas with different materials and play them.

Time of day: Small–group time

Materials:

- Plastic water bottles with caps
- Fillers, such as metal washers, beads, pebbles, sand, pennies, marbles, and (if your program allows the use of food other than for eating) rice, beans, or dried pasta
- Paper cups (to help children pour fillers into holders)

Curriculum content: KDI 41. Music. *Also:* KDI 17. Fine-motor skills

COR Advantage item: Y. Music. *Also:* item J. Fine-motor skills

Beginning: Have children close their eyes and listen. Shake a maraca (for example, filled with sand) and ask children to describe what they heard. Shake another maraca (for example, filled with pebbles) and ask children what was different about the two sounds. Explain to the children that this kind of instrument is called a maraca and that today they are going to make their own maracas. Give each child a basket with a water bottle and three types of fillers. Say something like "I wonder what you will put inside your maracas and how they will sound."

Middle: Move around the table, helping the children fill and fasten their maracas, if needed. Encourage them to try different holders and fillers. Also encourage children to move their maracas in different ways (shake, slide, twirl) and to listen to the sounds they make. Ask children to listen to the maracas others have made and guess what is inside them.

The chart at right offers an example, at each developmental level, of what children may say or do, along with ideas for scaffolding (supporting and gently extending) learning at each level. For additional ideas, refer to the scaffolding chart for Music on page 33. To read more about scaffolding, see page 20.

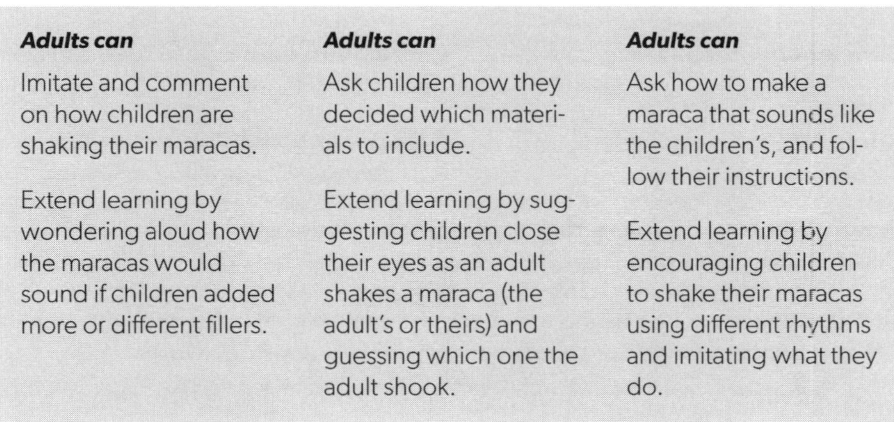

Scaffolding Learning at Each Developmental Level		
Earlier	**Middle**	**Later**
Children may	***Children may***	***Children may***
Fill their bottle with a few items and shake them to explore loud and soft or fast and slow.	Fill their bottles with one or more materials.	Make more than one maraca with different fillers.

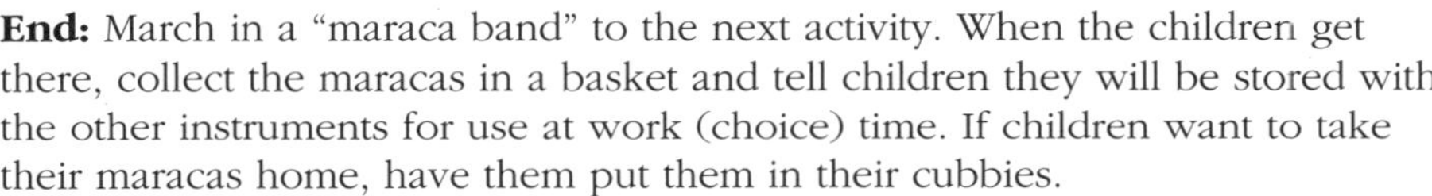

Earlier	**Middle**	**Later**
Adults can	***Adults can***	***Adults can***
Imitate and comment on how children are shaking their maracas.	Ask children how they decided which materials to include.	Ask how to make a maraca that sounds like the children's, and follow their instructions.
Extend learning by wondering aloud how the maracas would sound if children added more or different fillers.	Extend learning by suggesting children close their eyes as an adult shakes a maraca (the adult's or theirs) and guessing which one the adult shook.	Extend learning by encouraging children to shake their maracas using different rhythms and imitating what they do.

End: March in a "maraca band" to the next activity. When the children get there, collect the maracas in a basket and tell children they will be stored with the other instruments for use at work (choice) time. If children want to take their maracas home, have them put them in their cubbies.

Follow-up: Use the maracas at large-group time; for example, have children shake and move with them to different tempos of music. Use the maracas to give warnings before an activity ends — for example, go to each area near the end of work (choice) time and shake the maraca five times to indicate there are five more minutes left before cleanup time.

4 *Singing Your Feelings*

Summary description: Children sing about their feelings and act them out with facial expressions and movements.

Time of day: Large-group time

Materials:

None

Curriculum content: KDI 41. Music.
Also: KDI 9. Emotions

COR Advantage item: Y. Music.
Also: item D. Emotions

Beginning: Sing "If You're Happy and You Know It." Do the first action ("clap your hands") and have children imitate it. Ask children what they do to show they are happy, and sing "If you're happy and you know it" followed by their suggestions — which may be facial expressions (such as "smile" or "open my mouth wide") or movements (such as "jump" or "wiggle").

If you're happy and you know it, clap your hands [or other action; sing twice]

If you're happy and you know it, and you really have to show it

[Repeat first line]

Middle: Sing the words "If you're sad and you know it." Have children suggest facial expressions or movements and then sing the verse again while doing those actions. When children have the idea, encourage them to suggest emotions as well as actions. Encourage them to talk about each of the feelings.

The chart at right offers an example, at each developmental level, of what children may say and do, along with ideas for scaffolding (supporting and gently extending) children's learning at each level. For additional ideas, refer to the scaffolding chart for Music on page 33. To read more about scaffolding, see page 20.

Scaffolding Learning at Each Developmental Level

Earlier	Middle	Later
Children may	**Children may**	**Children may**
Observe (listen to) the others without joining in the singing or movements.	Sing most of the words and do all the expressions or actions, but not offer their own ideas.	Offer ideas for expressions or gestures to go along with the emotions adults name.
Adults can	**Adults can**	**Adults can**
Ask if children want to try one of the movements while accepting children's choice if they decide not to. Extend learning by encouraging children to watch what the adults and the other children are doing and by repeating the others' ideas; for example, "José says he stomps his feet when he's angry."	Nod encouragement as they perform the expressions or actions alongside children. Extend learning by asking "What do you do when you feel …" (naming a simple emotion such as happy, sad, or angry).	Repeat children's ideas and encourage the other children to make the expressions or gestures. Extend learning by encouraging children to suggest additional emotions to sing about and act out, and by talking about the things that make children feel a particular emotion; for example, "What makes you feel frustrated?"

End: Tell children you'll sing the song one more time, and ask them to suggest an emotion and an expression or action. Ask children how they feel when doing the next activity in the daily routine (for example, "How do you feel when we eat apple slices for snack?"), and tell them to move to that activity singing the appropriate verse accompanied by the expression or gesture that shows their feelings.

Follow-up: Sing other familiar songs for which children can substitute words and suggest actions or sounds — for example, "The Farmer in the Dell" (children suggest animals and make their sounds) or "The Wheels on the Bus" (children suggest what people or parts of the bus do, and act these out) For other examples, see "Animal Songs" (activity 10 in this chapter).

5

Listening for and Imitating Sounds

Summary description: Children take a walk to listen for sounds in the environment and imitate the sounds they hear.

Time of day: Large-group time, held outside

Materials:

None

Curriculum content: KDI 41. Music. *Also:* KDI 51. Natural and physical world, and KDI 58. Ecology

COR Advantage item: Y. Music. *Also:* item DD. Natural and physical world

Beginning: Tell the children that today they are going to take a walk to listen for sounds in the neighborhood. Soon after you start walking, stop with the children and ask what they hear. (Begin with an easily identified sound, such as a dog barking, a crow cawing, or a truck rumbling past.) Encourage children to identify the sound and imitate it.

Middle: As you continue walking, encourage children to listen for sounds coming from different directions and locations — for example, up in the sky. Encourage children to listen for sounds made by people, animals, vehicles, other equipment, and so on. You may need to remind children to listen now and then by saying something like "Let's be really quiet so we can hear."

The chart at right offers an example, at each developmental level, of what children may say and do, along with ideas for scaffolding (supporting and gently extending) children's learning. For additional ideas, refer to the scaffolding chart for Music on page 33. To read more about scaffolding, see page 20.

Scaffolding Learning at Each Developmental Level

Earlier	Middle	Later
Children may	***Children may***	***Children may***
Notice a sound and point to where it is coming from (e.g., in the sky or on the street).	Identify the sound they hear by saying something like "It's the garbage truck."	Describe and imitate the sounds they hear; for example, saying that the garbage truck is moving fast and going "Vroom!"
Adults can	***Adults can***	***Adults can***
Look to where children are pointing and acknowledge that they can hear the sound too. Extend learning by identifying the source of the sound, saying something like "It's a bird up in the tree" or "That's the train whistle."	Repeat the words or labels children use, and ask children to close their eyes and listen for other sounds. Extend learning by encouraging children to imitate the sounds they identify.	Ask children what else they can say about the sound. Extend learning by asking what sound the object or creature might make if it were doing something else; for example, "I wonder how the truck would sound if it were going slower" or "Suppose the bird were angry — what sound would it make then?"

End: As you return from your walk and get close to the school, tell the children to listen for one last sound. Have them reproduce that sound as they go inside and get ready for the next activity in the daily routine.

Follow-up: Repeat this activity when the weather is different (for example, on a windy day) and in different seasons (for example, in the spring, when children may hear more birds, or in the fall, when leaves and tall grasses rustle).

6

Bells, Bells, Bells

Summary description: Children explore different types of bells, using their hands and small tools to produce different sounds.

Time of day: Small-group time

Materials:

♦ A variety of bells such as hand bells, jingle bells, cow bells, resonator bells, and tubular bells (*Note:* For children who have trouble grasping the bells, attach them to their hands with velcro straps.)

♦ Tools made of wood, metal, and plastic — such as popsicle sticks, drum sticks, brushes with hard and soft bristles, spoons, rubber scrapers, pencils, and chopsticks

Curriculum content: KDI 41. Music. *Also:* KDI 52. Tools and technology, KDI 47. Experimenting, and KDI 48. Predicting

COR Advantage item: Y. Music. *Also:* item CC. Experimenting, predicting, and drawing conclusions

Beginning: Tell children that today they are going to play with bells. Ring one with your hands, using different motions, and invite the children to each try one. Hit your bell with a tool and encourage children to try a tool with their bell. Say something like "I notice that the bell makes a different kind of sound when I hit it with the spoon. I wonder how many different sounds we can make with the bells using our hands and these tools."

Middle: Name the different types of bells. Encourage children to explore the bells using different hand motions and tools — for example, by shaking, twirling, or sliding the bells, hitting the bells with their fingers, tapping the bells on the table, banging the bells with wooden or metal objects, and so on. Label children's actions. Talk about and compare the different sounds the bells make.

The chart at right offers an example, at each developmental level, of what children may say and do, along with ideas for scaffolding (supporting and gently extending) children's learning at each level. For additional ideas, refer to the scaffolding chart for Music on page 33. To read more about scaffolding, see page 20.

Scaffolding Learning at Each Developmental Level

Earlier	Middle	Later
Children may	**Children may**	**Children may**
Explore one or two bells using their hands.	Try a series of bells and/or tools.	Compare the sounds made by different bells and/or when using different tools.
Adults can	**Adults can**	**Adults can**
Imitate and describe children's actions. Extend learning by using one of the tools to make a sound with the bell and by encouraging children to try a tool with their bell.	Repeat the names of the types of bells and encourage children to describe the sounds each one makes. Extend learning by comparing — and encouraging children to compare — the sounds children make with different bells by using their hands and by using one or more tools.	Ask children to say which bell and tool they are using so the adults can try to make the same sound effects. Extend learning by encouraging children to predict the sounds that different bells will produce in combination with different tools; for example, adults can ask children how they think two types of bells will sound when hit with the same tool, or they can say something like "Do you think the ringing will be louder if you hit the bell with the wooden popsicle stick or the metal spoon?"

End: Tell children that small-group time will end after they try one more bell. Transition to the next activity by having each child carry (and ring) a bell to the area where musical instruments are stored. Remind children that they can continue to explore the bells at work (choice) time.

Follow-up: Use bells during planning and recall times. For example, put an area sign under each bell and have children choose and sound the bell that corresponds to the area in which they will play (or did play, if this activity is done during recall time). Provide sets of other instruments for children to explore during small-group time — for example, a set of percussion instruments that include drums, rhythm sticks, triangles, tambourines, cymbals, and a xylophone.

7

Parachute Pitches

Summary description: Children explore the range of their voice by modifying the pitch as they raise and lower a parachute.

Time of day: Large-group time

Materials:

Large parachute

Curriculum content: KDI 41. Music. *Also:* KDI 45. Observing, and KDI 46. Classifying

COR Advantage item: Y. Music. *Also:* item BB. Observing and classifying

Beginning: Stand in a circle with everyone holding on to a large parachute. Talk about low- and high-pitched sounds, and sing an example of each (exaggerate the difference with a very high and a very low pitch). Lower the parachute to the ground and encourage children to make the lowest sound they can. Raise the parachute and encourage them to produce a high pitch.

Middle: After the children have explored very high and very low pitches, lower the parachute slowly and encourage them to gradually lower the pitch of their voices. Do the same as you gradually raise the parachute. Ask children to suggest whether the parachute should be raised or lowered, and by how much (for example, all the way or partway), then to adjust the pitch of their voice accordingly.

The chart at right offers an example, at each developmental level, of what children may say and do, along with ideas for scaffolding (supporting and gently extending) children's learning. For additional ideas, refer to the scaffolding chart for Music on page 33. To read more about scaffolding, see page 20.

Scaffolding Learning at Each Developmental Level

Earlier	Middle	Later
Children may	**Children may**	**Children may**
Raise and lower the parachute without varying their voice.	Reproduce the highest and lowest pitches.	Slide their voice along the scale.
Adults can	**Adults can**	**Adults can**
Call children's attention to the sounds their classmates are making: "Let's listen to how our voices are changing as the parachute goes down (or up)." Extend learning by encouraging children to imitate the sounds they hear.	Label and imitate the sounds children make. Extend learning by encouraging children to pitch their voice "in between" two sounds and to play with sliding their voice up and down along the scale.	Start at a different pitch and have children raise and lower their voice from that note. Extend learning by asking children to suggest other ways to vary their voice as they move the parachute; for example, by making their voice softer as the parachute is lowered and gradually louder as the parachute is raised.

End: Tell the children you are going to raise and lower the parachute one more time, and ask them to suggest how to alter their voices. As you put away the parachute together, encourage the children to start outside with one pitch and end with a different pitch when they get back inside.

Follow-up: Explore other vocal variations that children can make as they raise and lower the parachute; for example, making continuous sounds as the parachute is lowered and making staccato sounds as it is raised. Move the parachute in other ways; for example, walk it around in a circle, and ask the children to suggest ways their voices can accompany the parachute's movements.

8   *Painting to Music*

Summary description: Children paint to express the feelings evoked by different types of music

Time of day: Small-group time

Materials:

- Paint, paper, and paintbrushes
- A few instrumental (lyric-free) music selections having different tempos (about three minutes per selection) and music player
- Paint smocks
- Sponges, paper towels, bowls of water, and so on for cleanup

Curriculum content: KDI 41. Music. *Also:* KDI 9. Emotions and KDI 17. Fine-motor skills

COR Advantage item: Y. Music. *Also:* item D. Emotions and item J. Fine-motor skills

Beginning: Tell children that today they are going to listen to different types of music and paint how the music makes them feel. Play the first selection (a slow, quiet piece) and ask the children what they notice about the music. Change to a contrasting piece (faster or louder) and ask how it differs from the first. Say something like "This music is faster, so I'm going to move my paintbrush fast too" or "I hear drums — I'm going to pretend my paintbrush is a drumstick, and drum on the paper." Demonstrate. Distribute painting supplies and replay the first piece of music. After three minutes, tell children you are going to change the music and play the second piece again.

Middle: Continue to play different types of music. Tell children they can paint on the same piece of paper or use a different paper for each piece. As you circulate among the children, describe — and encourage children to describe — the qualities of the music, children's motions with their brush, and the effects they create on the paper. Use words related to volume, tempo, pitch, and tonal qualities — for example, *loud, soft, fast, slow, high, low, smooth,* and *jumpy.*

The chart at right offers an example, at each developmental level, of what children may say and do, along with ideas for scaffolding (supporting and gently extending) children's learning at each level. For additional ideas, refer to the scaffolding chart for Music on page 33. To read more about scaffolding, see page 20.

Scaffolding Learning at Each Developmental Level

Earlier	Middle	Later
Children may	***Children may***	***Children may***
Explore paint materials without connecting it to the music.	Describe one or two qualities of the music — for example, they may say it is loud or fast.	Incorporate several qualities of the music in the brushwork, such as dots and lines for fast and slow, and zigzags and blobs for high and low pitches, respectively.
Adults can	***Adults can***	***Adults can***
Describe — and encourage children to describe — what they are doing; for example, "You are making the brush go around and around on the page." Gently extend learning by listening to and talking about the music's qualities. (*Note:* If children are intent on painting and do not want to attend to the music, respect their choice.)	Repeat children's descriptions and comment on how they capture those qualities in their brushwork: "You are moving the brush fast because the music is fast." Extend learning by using other descriptive terms and wondering aloud how children could paint them.	Comment on the variety of painting techniques children are using. Extend learning by introducing new vocabulary words (such as *flowing* or *staccato*) and by encouraging children to use their brushes in different ways to represent those musical qualities.

End: Let children know when you are about to play the last selection. Together with the children, clean up the painting supplies. For children who want to save their paintings or take them home, hang them up to dry. Put on a new music selection and tell children to move like the music to the next activity in the daily routine.

Follow-up: Have children represent musical qualities and ideas with other art media (for example, colored pencils, modeling clay, collage materials). Encourage children to talk about how the music makes them feel and what objects and events the sounds remind them of as they represent its features.

Singing Recall

Summary description: To the tune of "Did You Ever See a Lassie?" children share an object and sing about what they did at work (choice) time.

Time of day: Recall time

Materials:
♦ Paper bag
♦ Whatever toy each child places inside the bag that he or she played with at work (choice) time

Curriculum content: KDI 41. Music. *Also:* KDI 1. Initiative and KDI 6. Reflection

COR Advantage item: Y. Music. *Also:* item A. Initiative and planning and item C. Reflection

Beginning: Ask each child to put in the bag an object he or she played with at work (choice) time and bring it to recall. Tell the children that they are going to sing about the object and what they did with it to the tune of "Did You Ever See a Lassie?" (Children should already be familiar with the tune. If they are not, use another song they know well.) Sing an example through with the children; for example, "I played in the art area, art area, art area. I played in the art area and I used red paint."

Middle: As children recall, encourage them to add more details by singing another verse. For example, suggest they sing about what they did with the hammer, or say something like "You solved a problem with the tape when it got tangled. Sing how you did that."

The chart at right offers an example, at each developmental level, of what children may say and do, along with ideas for scaffolding (supporting and gently extending) children's learning at each level. For additional ideas, refer to the scaffolding chart for Music on page 33. To read more about scaffolding, see page 20.

Scaffolding Learning at Each Developmental Level

Earlier	Middle	Later
Children may	***Children may***	***Children may***
Name the object without singing.	Sing one thing about the object or what they did with it, using the melody for part of the time and random pitches for the rest.	Keep the tune for the entire recall.
Adults can	***Adults can***	***Adults can***
Acknowledge and repeat what children say. Extend learning by singing a simple verse of the song; for example, "You played in the house area, house area (etc.) … and you made pizza."	Sing a verse through with children. Extend learning by encouraging children to add more details to their recall.	Encourage the other children to listen to the children who are able to keep the tune while singing about what they did. Extend learning by asking children to keep adding verses with additional details and by asking if they would like to make up their own tune.

End: After everyone has recalled, have them put their objects away. Then, using the same tune, sing where in the daily routine everyone will be going next; for example, "We're going to snacktime, snacktime, etc.," and ask the children to suggest the last line — "Where we will …."

Follow-up: At planning time, have children sing about the area in which they plan to play and about what they will do there. For both planning and recall versions of this activity, try different tunes that the children are familiar with. For example, to "Twinkle, Twinkle, Little Star," a child could sing "I played in the house area, house area, house area. I played in the house area, and I ___________."

10 — *Animal Songs*

Summary description: To the tune of "The Wheels on the Bus," children name and sing animal sounds.

Time of day: Large-group time

Materials:
None

Curriculum content: KDI 41. Music. *Also:* KDI 46. Classifying and KDI 51. Natural and physical world

COR Advantage item: Y. Music. *Also:* item BB. Observing and classifying and item DD. Natural and physical world

Beginning: To the tune of "The Wheels on the Bus," sing "The lion likes to sing this song, sing this song, sing this song. The lion likes to sing this song. Roar, roar, roar." Encourage the children to sing it through two more times with you.

Middle: Ask children, in turn, to name an animal and the sound it makes. Using their answers, sing each verse through at least twice with the children. They may want to add body movements, such as jumping like monkeys or hopping like rabbits. If they don't know what sound an animal makes, encourage them to invent one; for example, you might say, "I wonder what sound a tiny ant makes."

The chart at right offers an example, at each developmental level, of what children may may say and do, along with ideas for scaffolding (supporting and gently extending) learning at each level. For additional ideas, refer to the scaffolding chart for Music on page 33. To read more about scaffolding, see page 20.

Scaffolding Learning at Each Developmental Level		
Earlier	**Middle**	**Later**
Children may	***Children may***	***Children may***
Observe and occasionally sing part of the song or perform an action.	Sing all the words and perform the motions but not volunteer their own ideas.	Offer their own ideas as well as copy those of others.
Adults can	***Adults can***	***Adults can***
Comment on children's behavior: "Jules, you're hissing like a snake." Extend learning by suggesting children might want to move like the animal too.	Sing and move alongside children. Extend learning by asking children if they want to suggest an animal sound or movement, and accept their choice if they don't want to.	Repeat children's ideas and encourage the class to copy them. Extend learning by asking how the animal would make that sound if it were happy (or sad, angry, hungry, and so on), and then sing the same verse, varying the tone of voice according to children's response (e.g., the lion might roar louder if it were angry or the cow might moo longer if she were hungry).

End: Alert the children when you are about to sing the last verse. When the activity is over, tell them to make sounds and move like one of the animals they sang about as they go to the next activity in the daily routine.

Follow-up: Have children substitute animal sounds (and motions) using other familiar songs. For example, to the tune of "Frère Jacques," sing "I'm a chicken. I'm a chicken. Hear me cluck. Hear me cluck. Cluck, cluck, cluck, cluck. Cluck, cluck. cluck, cluck. I'm a chicken. Hear me cluck." Instead of animals, you can use vehicles or other categories of interest to the children.

Activities for

Movement

During the 47 years I've been bouncing around the education field, we have danced and moved to depict ... all the king's horses racing to help Humpty Dumpty; the transformations of caterpillar to butterfly, tadpole to frog; the dynamic pageant of moving seasons; the wheels of the bus on the way to the zoo; number facts and spelling words ... Every idea is a universe of possibilities (Chenfeld, 2005, pp. 50–51).

The Development of Movement in Children

Young children take great pleasure in expressing themselves through creative movement — that is, "taking a familiar movement and changing it in some way" (Sawyers, Colley, & Icaza, 2010, p. 32). Preschoolers love to experiment and invent new ways to use their bodies. They imitate the actions of peers, meet movement challenges ("How can you move to the table without using your feet?"), and set creative tests for themselves ("Watch how low I can walk. How high!").

Children need little encouragement to move. Infants and toddlers eagerly master basic mobility skills. Preschoolers, who move with greater coordination and confidence, are freer to push their physical limits in new directions. Their attempts are self-regulating in the sense that their bodies provide instant feedback. They know when they succeed — they

remain upright, get where they want to go, or inspire others to copy them. Likewise, they can tell when they are not accomplishing their goals — they lose their balance, miss their mark, or can't get their ideas across. When this happens, they problem solve with their bodies until their actions match the image in their mind.

Despite this strong inner drive to move creatively, research shows that young children can be surprisingly limited in the numbers of ways they use their bodies. For example, while listening to music, three-year-olds are likely to move in place, while children aged four and five tend to move up and down, side to side, or in circles (Sims, 1985). It often takes an adult issuing a creative challenge for preschoolers to move in other than familiar or prescribed ways. "A child is unlikely to look at the jungle gym and decide to pretend to be clothes hanging on the line to dry; but a play leader — someone who interacts with children by asking leading questions and providing guidance for certain skills ... without taking charge — can suggest such an activity" (Pica, 2011, p. 58).

It is their growing ability to understand language, and to hold images of objects, people, and actions in mind, that allows preschoolers to use movement as a form of creative representation. They can stand tall and lumber like a giant, float through the air like a balloon, or careen around the room like a car. Conveying their feelings, experiences, and ideas through movement builds young children's confidence in their ability to communicate with their bodies. This sense of bodily comfort and creativity in movement spills over into other areas of learning and strengthens children's belief in themselves as academically capable, socially competent, and imaginative young people (Centers for Disease Control, 2010). In fact, like all the other creative arts, expressive movement can be connected to virtually every area of the preschool curriculum.

For example, studies show that participating in movement activities improves children's ability to follow instructions, listen for cues, and respect the needs of others in a shared space (Dow, 2010). "During creative movement, children learn to think before they act, pay attention to detail, and consider differences between experiences" (Marigliano & Russo, 2011, p. 48). These observations are confirmed by brain research, which yields results similar to those discovered with music training. Neurological studies find that movement and exercise can spark the growth of new brain cells and facilitate learning. Movement improves alertness, attention, and motivation and encourages nerve cells to bind to one another, which is the basis for logging in new information (Ratey, 2008). The ability to move to a steady beat has been linked to auditory brainstem responses related to language development (Tierney & Kraus, 2013); children who are at risk for language and literacy delays improved their reading skills after training to synchronize their movement to a steady beat. Finally, movement experiences spill over to other aspects of creative activity. Experimenting with movement enhances the ability to think fluently, develop original ideas, and begin to deal with abstractions (Bradley, 2002). Put another way, young children learn to turn ideas around in their head, improvise, and think in images from different angles.

Materials and Equipment That Support Movement

Children's explorations with movement will be enhanced when they work with the following equipment and materials:

- Varied instrumental musical selections
- Instruments to hold and move with (tambourines, maracas)
- Scarves, ribbons, streamers
- Tarps, sheets, and blankets to pull, twirl, and go over and under
- Paper plates
- Hoops
- Limbo sticks
- Rubber tires
- Materials children can throw and kick in creative ways (bean bags, balls)
- Equipment children can safely climb, and hang and jump from, using different body positions (tire swings, ramps, steps, boards, low balance beams, mattresses, hula hoops)

For additional ideas, see *The HighScope Preschool Curriculum* (Epstein & Hohmann, 2012, Chapter 6, pp. 171–221).

Teaching Strategies That Support Movement

Teachers can encourage movement throughout the day by putting these ideas into practice:

Describe — and encourage children to describe — their creative uses of movement.

Comment on the different ways children move throughout the day. For example, you might see a child balancing an object on his or her head to carry it across the room, or galloping downhill at outside time. Label and describe the movement, and invite children to do the same.

Encourage children to solve movement problems at group times and transitions.

Children naturally solve movement problems as they play — for example, how to turn a corner while riding on a tricycle. They also enjoy figuring out problems that adults set for them; for example, how many ways they can move over, under, or around a low table. Meeting such challenges exercises young children's creativity.

Provide opportunities for children to represent their experiences through movement.

Movement, like the other arts, offers a way for preschoolers to represent objects and actions. Encourage them to use movement in pretend play ("I wonder how the dog will move when it's tired"). Ask children to act out during recall what they did at work time, move like a character in a book or story as they transition to the next activity, or reenact a field-trip experience.

Encourage simple ways of moving creatively to music.

Hearing music makes children want to move. Provide a variety of musical styles — fast and slow, bouncy and smooth, continuous or syncopated — so children can match their movements to different sounds. Offer props, such as streamers or scarves, to enhance children's creative options. Imitate, label, and describe how they move to music, and encourage them to observe and comment on the movements of others. For more information on teaching strategies that support movement in preschool, see Epstein (2012, Chapter 5.)

Incorporating Cultural Diversity in Movement

Movement, with or without musical accompaniment, is often associated with distinctive cultural beliefs and rituals. Use photos, short clips, and where possible, live performances to expose children to different ways of moving for entertainment or ceremonial purposes. Provide props used in dances or rituals for children to explore at large-group time and add them to the dress-up items in the house area.

Movement is also a part of daily routines, such as the way a parent rocks a child, how we carry our bodies, or the actions we use to scrape dirty dishes or scrub our hands. Ask families to think about the ways they move at home, including the spontaneous dances they do around the house or at religious celebrations and other gatherings. You, and they, may be surprised at the diversity of movements uncovered by these reflections. Below are some ideas to get you started.

Performers. You might talk about, and provide samples of, work by the following artists: Maria Tallchief (Native American dancer); Misty

Copeland (African-American dancer); Gregory Hines (African-American tap dancer); Alvin Ailey (African-American choreographer); Bill T. Jones (African-American choreographer); Judith Jamison (African-American dancer); Sara Baras (Flamenco dancer); Yuan Yuan Tan (Chinese dancer); Alicia Alonso (Cuban dancer and choreographer); Mikhail Baryshnikov (Russian dancer); Anna Pavlova (Russian dancer); Uday Shankar (Indian dancer and choreographer).

Genres. The following are dance styles and rhythms you could introduce children to, which together reflect a diversity of cultures and influences: salsa (Cuba); country-western line dancing; tap dancing; hip-hop and break dancing; polka (Scandinavia); Yangko (China); Balinese dancing (Indonesia); belly dancing (Middle East); tango (Argentina); Ramvong (Cambodia); dragon dance (China); Merengue (Dominican Republic); step dancing (Ireland); Hora (Israel); Noh (Japan); troika (Russia); jig and reel (Scotland); Kathak (India); Morris dancing (U.K.); Native American ceremonial dances.

Materials. You could introduce children to the following items, which are used with creative movement in different cultures: finger cymbals; maracas; "swirling" skirts and robes; woven and printed scarves; hoops; maypole with streamers; hard-soled boots; tap shoes; feathers; masks; paper fans; cloth or leather strips with bells (to hold in hands or tie around wrists and ankles); lengths of fringe.

Adapting Movement Materials and Activities for Children With Special Needs

Children with limited mobility can participate in movement activities by using functioning body parts and augmenting their physical abilities with assistive devices. Seeing how children with special needs express themselves through movement will also inspire classmates to use a broader range of body parts and actions in their own creative movements. Try the following ideas and look toward the children in your program for additional adaptations.

- Provide ample room for children with and without mobility devices to move.

- Remove and/or securely fasten down anything that might get caught in mobility devices.

- Remove and/or pad the edges of anything sharp or protruding (as you would for *all* children).

- Encourage children who cannot move their whole body to move the parts they can — for example, to wave their arms, swivel their shoulders, or change the direction their head is turned.

- Children can use the parts of their body they can move, or partner with another child to create a shape or letter, instead of trying to make shapes or letters with their whole body.

- Encourage children to use their available body parts in making up movement or dance stories.

- Encourage children to collaborate with "able-bodied" peers for an activity in which each child provides one or more body parts to create a movement — for example, one child is the "arms" and the other child is the "legs."

- For moving with objects, such as streamers or paper plates, attach them to children's hands with Velcro straps or elastic bands.

Adapting Movement Materials and Activities for Children Who Are Dual Language Learners (DLLs)

Movement naturally lends itself to description and thus becomes a useful tool for enhancing receptive language (the ability to understand spoken and written language) and encouraging expressive vocabulary in English. Try the ideas listed below to help DLL children build their linguistic skills through the creative use of movement.

- Encourage children to name and describe, in their home language, their body parts and creative movements, and provide the English equivalent.

- Label movement equipment and materials in the language(s) children in the classroom speak, as well as in English.

- Encourage DLL children and native English speakers to collaborate during movement activities, sharing their discoveries and ideas, and helping one another solve problems.

- Encourage DLL children to be leaders and demonstrators during movement activities that do not require language. Having others watch and follow their lead will build confidence that will transfer to trying out their emerging language skills.

- Partner DLLs with native English speakers during movement activities. Act as a translator to help them understand and carry out one another's ideas. Check with DLL children to make sure you have correctly understood and communicated their ideas. Check with native English speakers to make sure they understand the DLL children's intentions.

- Learn the names of movements (run, jump, swing, bend) and body parts (arms, legs, neck) in children's home language(s) and use them together with English words to describe creative movements.

1   *Story Movements*

> **Summary description:** Children move their bodies in different ways as they act out a story.

Time of day: Large-group time

Materials:
None

Curriculum content: KDI 42. Movement. *Also:* KDI 16. Gross-motor skills

COR Advantage item: Z. Movement. *Also:* item I. Gross-motor skills

Beginning: Explain to the children that you are going to tell a story and they are going to act it out as you tell it. Begin a story that involves moving in different ways, such as creeping through a forest, rolling in the sand, or swimming in the ocean. For example, you might begin, "Sara and Sayed went with their family on a trip to the beach. First, they set down their blankets. (Pause for the children to act this out.) Then, Sara and Sayed ran down the sand to the ocean. (Pause.) But — ouch! The sand was hot on the bottoms of their feet because the sun was shining on it." (Pause.)

Middle: Continue to make up the story (for example, describing diving in the water, splashing, swimming away from a shark), pausing often for children to invent the accompanying movements. Ask the children to contribute their ideas to the story ("We're running away from a crocodile!") and move to their ideas. Encourage them to label (name) and describe their movements, and to watch and imitate one another.

The chart at right offers an example, at each developmental level, of what children may say or do, along with ideas for scaffolding (supporting and gently extending) children's learning at each level. For additional ideas, refer to the scaffolding chart for Movement on page 34. To read more about scaffolding see page 20.

Scaffolding Learning at Each Developmental Level

Earlier	Middle	Later
Children may	***Children may***	***Children may***
Move their bodies in ways unrelated to the story.	Move in simple ways to represent the story.	Move in complex ways to represent the story; for example, they may slither along the floor, kick their legs, and make swimming motions with their arms.
Adults can	***Adults can***	***Adults can***
Label and imitate children's actions: "You're taking big steps — I'm going to do that too." Extend learning by commenting on other children's movements and encouraging children to copy those as well: "Daria is pretending to drag her feet through wet sand — maybe you'd like to try that with me too."	Comment on how children's movements are related to the narrative: "You're sliding on the floor to show you're swimming." Extend learning by asking children to describe their movements and connect them to the story: "Tell me what you're doing now; what part of the story is that?"	Ask for directions so they can copy children's movements: "Tell me how to move my arms and legs like yours." Extend learning by presenting children with additional challenges (e.g., saying something like "Suppose the waves suddenly got really high — how would you move then?") and encouraging children to add their own challenging elements to the story.

End: Bring the story to an end; for example, have the characters pack up to leave the beach (or return home or go back to their school). Pick an element from the story (for example, swimming in the water) and have the children move that way to the next activity in the daily routine.

Follow-up: Using a familiar book as the starting point for a story, encourage children to change the story or make up what comes next and then create accompanying movements. At recall time, have children repeat a movement they used at work time and then tell what they did.

2

Glued to the Floor

Summary description: Children pretend that parts of their bodies are glued to the floor and invent ways to move with that part fixed in place.

Time of day: Large-group time

Materials:
None

Curriculum content: KDI 42. Movement. *Also:* KDI 16. Gross-motor skills and KDI 18. Body awareness

COR Advantage item: Z. Movement. *Also:* item I. Gross-motor skills

Beginning: Tell children that they are going to pretend part of their body is "glued to the floor" and they have to figure out how to move the rest of their body with that part fixed in place. Model this for children by bending or crouching and putting your hands on the floor. Then move — for example, stretch one leg to the side and describe what you are doing: "I can't move my hands, so I'm stretching my leg." Tell the children to glue their hands to the floor; then say something like "I wonder how you will move another part of your body."

Middle: Comment on which body parts children move and how they move them; for example, you might say, "Rowan is shaking her head" or "Jaffar is twisting his feet." Ask children to suggest another body part to glue to the floor. Encourage them to share ideas and imitate one another.

The chart at right offers an example, at each developmental level, of what children may say and do, along with ideas for scaffolding (supporting and gently extending) children's learning at each level. For additional ideas, refer to the scaffolding chart for Movement on page 34. To read more about scaffolding, see page 20.

Scaffolding Learning at Each Developmental Level

Earlier	Middle	Later
Children may	**Children may**	**Children may**
Move the body part that is supposed to be glued to the floor as they move other parts.	Move other body parts in one or two ways while keeping the designated part glued.	Move their bodies in several ways while keeping the designated part stuck to the floor.
Adults can	**Adults can**	**Adults can**
Comment on the other body parts children are moving; for example, children may be turning their heads or wiggling their butts. Extend learning by saying something like "I wonder how you could turn your head with your hands still stuck on the floor."	Imitate children's movements and describe — and encourage children to describe — how they are moving. Extend learning by wondering if there are other ways children could move while still keeping the designated part glued to the floor and by encouraging them to observe, copy, and change the ways that other children are moving.	Comment on the different ways children are moving; for example, if the children's feet are stuck to the floor, by saying "Matilda, first you twisted your whole body from side to side, then you stretched your hands over your head, and now you're bending your knees." Extend learning by suggesting children think of two body parts to glue to the floor at the same time and seeing how many different ways they can still move.

End: Tell the children there is time to glue one last body part to the floor today. Have them move to the next activity in the routine holding one part of their body stiff; that is, fixed in one position.

Follow-up: Use the transition activity described in "End," above (moving the rest of the body while holding one or more parts stiff) as a large-group activity. Ask children to pretend there is a magnet pulling one body part across the room and they have to move with that part in the lead. At other large-group times, have children move as if they are walking through mud, through sand, or on hot pavement.

3   *Slinky Movements*

Summary description: Children explore ways to move a Slinky® with their hands, with other parts of their bodies, and with a partner.

Time of day: Large-group time

Materials:
One Slinky per person

Curriculum content: KDI 42. Movement. *Also:* KDI 12. Building relationships and KDI 18. Body awareness

COR Advantage item: Z. Movement. *Also:* item F. Building relationships with other children

Beginning: Tell the children that today they are going to explore a toy called a Slinky. Stretch the Slinky with your hands. Give each child a Slinky and ask children to see how they can make it move.

Middle: After the children have moved the Slinky using their hands, suggest that they make it move using other parts of their bodies, such as their elbows, pinkies or thumbs only, feet, knees, head, stomach, or backside. Suggest they also work with a partner, stretching the Slinky between them. Describe — and encourage children to describe — what they are doing.

The chart at right offers an example, at each developmental level, of what children may say and do, along with ideas for scaffolding (supporting and gently extending) learning at each level. For additional ideas, refer to the scaffolding chart for Movement on page 34. To read more on scaffolding, see page 20.

Scaffolding Learning at Each Developmental Level

Earlier	Middle	Later
Children may	***Children may***	***Children may***
Stretch the Slinky to different lengths using both hands.	Explore the Slinky with one or both hands and with their fingers.	Move the Slinky with several body parts and in several different ways; for example, they may scoot it along the floor with their knees, wrap it around their waists, or stretch t from the floor to the too of their heads (to match their height).
Adults can	***Adults can***	***Adults can***
Stretch their Slinky to match children's and comment on the length — "I'm making mine long (or short) like yours" — and use words like *stretch*, *pull*, and *coil*. Extend learning by saying something like "I wonder how you could move the Slinky with just one hand or just certain fingers" and suggesting to children that they try movements other than stretching — for example, twisting or jiggling the Slinky.	Describe — and encourage children to describe — their actions: "You hooked your pinkies in the ends and pulled them out to the sides." Extend learning by encouraging children to try moving the Slinky with other parts of their body, saying, for example, "How could you make the Slinky move using your feet or your elbows?" and asking children what they could do with the Slinky other than stretching it.	Imitate all the ways children use the Slinky, and ask them to repeat their actions on adults (e.g., coiling the Slinky around an adult's wrist). Extend learning by encouraging children to work with a partner: "Suppose you and Aiden each held one end?"

End: Give the children a warning when the activity time is nearing its end; then put the Slinkies away, reminding children that they will be available at work (choice) time. Tell the children to move like a Slinky on the way to the next activity in the routine.

Follow-up: Encourage children to explore using the Slinkies on and with different objects and equipment; for example, on block structures they erect. Bring the Slinkies outside for children to use with equipment and natural features, such as the bottom of the slide, steps of the ladder, rungs of the climber, low and high hills, boulders, tree stumps, and so on.

4

Start and Stop Body Statues

Summary description: Children "freeze" in different statue positions each time the music stops.

Time of day: Large-group time

Materials:

♦ Music player you can easily start and stop
♦ Recording(s) of instrumental music

Curriculum content: KDI 42. Movement. *Also:* KDI 18. Body awareness and KDI 41. Music

COR Advantage item: Z. Movement. *Also:* item Y. Music

Beginning: Tell the children that today they will be playing a game that involves making statues. Explain that a statue is solid and cannot move. Demonstrate a pose and then ask children to hold their body "frozen" like a statue, without moving. Tell them that you're going to play some music and they can move however they'd like but that, when the music stops, they must freeze like a statue. Start the music and, after several seconds, hit the pause button. Remind children to freeze.

Middle: Describe children's body positions; for example, you might say, "Jonah's statue has its leg to the side," or "Renee's statue is hunkered down low." Encourage children to move expressively to the music. Before starting the music each time, remind children that they can move when the music starts but that, when it stops, they have to freeze again. Encourage them to freeze with their bodies in a different shape than the one they made the last time. Have each child choose a movement (and frozen position) for others to copy.

The chart at right offers an example, at each developmental level, of what children may say and do, along with ideas for scaffolding (supporting and gently extending) children's learning at each level. For additional ideas, refer to the scaffolding chart for Movement on page 34. To read more about scaffolding, see page 20.

Scaffolding Learning at Each Developmental Level		
Earlier	**Middle**	**Later**
Children may	***Children may***	***Children may***
Start and stop moving without synchronizing their actions to the music.	Freeze in one or two ways each time.	Experiment with different ways of balancing (freezing) their bodies.
Adults can	***Adults can***	***Adults can***
Occasionally repeat the directions to "freeze when the music stops," but without expecting chidren to follow this or pressuring them to do so. Extend learning by saying something like "I wonder what kind of statue you will make when I stop the music this time."	Label and imitate children's positions: "I'm standing with my arms over my head just like you." Extend learning by saying something like "I wonder if you will freeze a different way next time" and encouraging children to look at the ways other children are freezing.	Comment on what children did last time and what they are doing differently this time. Extend learning by giving children movement challenges, such as asking "What else could you do with your arms when you freeze?"

End: Tell children you will play and stop the music one more time. Tell children to pretend they are a frozen statue that is "melting" as they move to the next activity.

Follow-up: Encourage children to create their own start-and-stop movement games at outside time. Use actual instruments or things other than recorded music (for example, a loud tapping or scraping noise) to signal starting and stopping. At cleanup time, tell children to momentarily "freeze" and then to resume cleaning up.

5   *Obstacle Course*

> **Summary description:** Children create and move in different ways around an obstacle course.

Time of day: Large-group time

Materials:

Objects that children can navigate over, under, around, and through, such as inner tubes or tires; hula hoops; balance beams; hollow or wooden blocks (stacked up, in rows on the floor, making a low wall); large empty cartons (from appliances); construction cones; and empty coffee cans turned upside down (to step on) or right side up (to step in)

Curriculum content: KDI 42. Movement. *Also:* KDI 16. Gross-motor skills, KDI 18. Body awareness, and KDI 35. Spatial awareness

COR Advantage item: Z. Movement. *Also:* item I. Gross-motor skills and item T. Geometry: Shapes and spatial awareness

Beginning: Set up an obstacle course beginning with three objects that invite different types of movement — for example, three hula hoops, a balance beam, and an empty carton. Tell the children that this is called an obstacle course and that today they are going to move through it in different ways. Demonstrate and label going over, under, around, and/or through the objects. Invite the children to move through the course in their own ways. (*Note:* To minimize collisions, set up the course with a beginning and end point, and encourage children to move in the same direction by returning to the starting point when they get to the end. Use conflicts over space as an opportunity to problem solve with the children.)

Middle: Ask the children for their ideas about other objects to add to the obstacle course. As you and they move through the course, continue to emphasize spatial concepts such as *over, under, through, around,* and *between.* Use familiar position and direction words (*on top of, below, forward, backward*) and introduce new ones (*ahead, behind*). Encourage children to move in straight lines, make zigzag paths, hold their bodies high or low, and otherwise experiment with what their bodies can do. Suggest they make up creative ways to move for others to copy.

The chart at right offers an example, at each developmental level, of what children may say and do, along with ideas for scaffolding (supporting and gently extending) children's learning at each level. For additional ideas, refer to the scaffolding chart for Movement on page 34. To read more about scaffolding, see page 20.

Scaffolding Learning at Each Developmental Level		
Earlier	**Middle**	**Later**
Children may	***Children may***	***Children may***
Move (e.g., walk) from point to point without navigating in different ways around the objects.	Use one or two types of movements, regardless of the object; for example, they may attempt to step over everything.	Try different types of movements as they navigate around the obstacle course.
Adults can	***Adults can***	***Adults can***
Describe how and where children are moving: "You're walking from the construction cone to the stack of blocks." Extend learning by starting at the same point and demonstrating a way of moving around (under, through, etc.) the object and then doing the same for the next object, also using position and direction words to describe what they are doing, and inviting children to imitate (while accepting children's choice not to, if they don't).	Imitate children's actions. Extend learning by saying something like "I wonder how else you could move when you get to the (object)" and encouraging children to see how others navigate when they get to that object and to try out those movements themselves.	Imitate and label children's actions, emphasizing what is different about each one: "You jumped over the row of blocks but walked around the tower." Extend learning by suggesting movement challenges: "How could you get to the other side of the hula hoop without standing up?"

End: Tell children they can each go through the obstacle course one more time. Together with the children, return the obstacles to their regular storage places. Have children pretend there is an obstacle they must get past (such as a balance beam or a big hole in the floor) as they navigate their way to the next activity in the routine.

Follow-up: Repeat this activity with increasingly difficult obstacles. Invite family members to contribute objects that can be used as obstacles. Encourage children to create and move around obstacle courses outside.

6

Step Aerobics With Blocks

Summary description: Children move their legs and feet in different ways while doing "step aerobics" with a block, alone and/or together with other children.

Time of day: Large-group time

Materials:
Hollow or wooden blocks, 12" x 24" x 4" (one block per person)

Curriculum content: KDI 42. Movement. *Also:* KDI 13. Cooperative play and KDI 16. Gross-motor skills

COR Advantage item: Z. Movement. *Also:* item F. Building relationships with other children and item I. Gross-motor skills

Beginning: Explain the activity to children, saying something like "Today we are going to move our bodies in different ways — up, down, over and around a block." Demonstrate one way of moving; for example, start behind the block and step up, then step back down. Demonstrate another way — for example, step up and then off to the side. Say something like "Let's see what ideas you have for moving up, down, around, and over the block."

Middle: Circulate around the room as children experiment with ways of moving their body using the block. Use position and direction words to label their actions (for example, *up*, *down*, *sideways*, *behind*, *in front of*, *over*, and *around*). Encourage children to take turns imitating one another and/or to combine their blocks (for example, in a stack or row) and to invent ways of moving together.

The chart at right offers an example, at each developmental level, of what children may say and do, along with ideas for scaffolding (supporting and gently extending) children's learning at each level. For additional ideas, refer to the scaffolding chart for Movement on page 34. To read more about scaffolding, see page 20.

Scaffolding Learning at Each Developmental Level		
Earlier	**Middle**	**Later**
Children may	***Children may***	***Children may***
Move in one or two ways (e.g., stepping up and back down, stepping up and forward).	Move in several ways (e.g., jumping over the block, balancing on one foot, alternating which side they step off on).	Move in many ways (e.g., stepping up and turning around; bending over the block, putting their hands on the floor, then lifting their legs over; straddling the block).
Adults can	***Adults can***	***Adults can***
Label and imitate children's actions. Extend learning by demonstrating and naming other ways of moving, such as moving sideways or going around the block, and inviting children to try these ideas (while acceptingchildren's choice if they don't).	Describe — and encourage children to describe — children's actions. Extend learning with movement challenges: "How could you get to the other side of the block without lifting your feet?"	Recognize children's ideas by labeling children's actions. Extend learning by encouraging children to work with one another: "Suppose you and Jamie shared one block — how could you move together (or take turns)?"

End: Tell children to think of one more way to move over, under, or around their block. Together with the children, put the blocks away, and remind children that they can continue to invent ways to move at work (choice) time. Tell them to imagine there is a great big block in the middle of the room that they must navigate (get over, under, around, or through) as they move to the next activity in the daily routine.

Follow-up: Do this same activity with other physical props such as a hula hoop, inner tube, milk crate, balance beam, or large carton. Add music for children to practice "stepping to the beat."

7

Massage Rollers

Summary description: Children think of different places on their body where they can use a massage roller, as well as how to maneuver their body to get to hard-to-reach places.

Time of day: Large-group time

Materials:

Various types of handheld massage rollers

Curriculum content: KDI 42. Movement. *Also:* KDI 4. Problem solving and KDI 18. Body awareness

COR Advantage item: Z. Movement. *Also:* item B. Problem solving with materials

Beginning: Show children the rollers, and point out that each has a place they can hold on to and a part that rolls. Demonstrate using the roller — for example, by rolling it up and down your arm. Ask where else you could roll it on your body, and try out one or two of the children's ideas. Give each child a roller and say "I wonder where you will use your rollers."

Middle: Encourage children to think of all the different places on their bodies where they can use the roller. Challenge them to reach unusual places; for example, you might say, "How could you use it on the bottom of your feet without falling down?" or "How can you reach your back (or the back of your neck)?" Suggest that, instead of moving the roller on their body, they put it in a fixed position (on the table or floor, protruding from a shelf) and move their body along the roller.

The chart at right offers an example, at each developmental level, of what children may say and do, along with ideas for scaffolding (supporting and gently extending) children's learning at each level. For additional ideas, refer to the scaffolding chart for Movement on page 34. To read more about scaffolding, see page 20.

Scaffolding Learning at Each Developmental Level

Earlier	Middle	Later
Children may	***Children may***	***Children may***
Use the roller on the same parts and in the same way that adults demonstrate.	Use the roller in different ways on one body part and then try it on other easy-to-reach parts.	Explore many different ways of using the rollers with their body.
Adults can	***Adults can***	***Adults can***
Imitate and describe children's actions. Extend learning by moving their roller a different way on that same body part and seeing if children imitate.	Describe — and encourage children to describe — all the body parts involved and all the ways they are using the roller. Extend learning by wondering how children could use the roller on harder-to-reach places and/or keep the roller fixed while moving only their body.	Offer children additional challenges involving other parts of their own body or other positions for the rollers. Extend learning by wondering how children could use their rollers on one another's body (with permission), either by taking turns or by trying to massage each other at the same time.

End: Tell children to explore two more ways to use the rollers. Put the rollers away, and tell children they can continue to play with them at work (choice) time and outside time. Tell them to pretend their arm is a massage roller and to use it on a part of their body as they move to the next activity in the daily routine.

Follow-up: Use massage rollers together with music at large-group time. Encourage children to move the rollers in different ways depending on the musical selections you play. At small-group time, give each child a roller and a doll or stuffed animal to massage in different ways.

8   *Body Parts and Music*

Summary description: While listening to music, children explore all the ways they can move one part of their body, then a different part, then two parts at the same time.

Time of day: Large-group time

Materials:

Music player with various selections of different instrumental music

Curriculum content: KDI 42. Movement. *Also:* KDI 16. Gross-motor skills KDI 18. Body awareness, and KDI 35. Spatial awareness

COR Advantage item: Z. Movement. *Also:* item I. Gross-motor skills and item T. Geometry: Shapes and spatial awareness

Beginning: Play a piece of instrumental music (for example, something slow) and say "I'm going to move just my arm to the music." Move your arm in slow circles or wave it back and forth in front of your chest. Encourage the children to move their arm to the music. Change the music (for example, to a march) and move your arm a different way — for example, in chopping motions up and down. Say something like "Let's see how you move your arm to this music."

Middle: Play each selection for about three minutes as children move their arms in different ways. Then play a new selection (or repeat an earlier one) and ask children to suggest a different body part to move. Later still, have children move two body parts to the music. Encourage them to describe each movement using position and direction words.

The chart at right offers an example, at each developmental level, of what children may say and do, along with ideas for scaffolding (supporting and gently extending) children's learning. For additional ideas, refer to the scaffolding chart for Movement on page 34. To read more about scaffolding, see page 20.

Scaffolding Learning at Each Developmental Level

Earlier	Middle	Later
Children may	***Children may***	***Children may***
Repeat the same movement with the same body part for each musical selection.	Move each body part in two or three ways.	Move each body part in many ways and describe what they are doing.
Adults can	***Adults can***	***Adults can***
Imitate and describe children's actions.	Encourage children to label (name) their movements and repeat the action, position, and direction words they use; encourage children to observe what other children are doing and to share their ideas with their peers.	Suggest children invent combinations for using two body parts at once (e.g., moving the arm and leg on the same side of their body) and encourage children to name two body parts to move and to describe their actions.
Extend learning by saying something like "How else could you move your arm?" and when the music changes, commenting that the music sounds different: "I wonder how you will move your arm now."	Extend learning by having adults close their eyes and asking children to describe the movements they are making so the adults can make those movements too, and by introducing new vocabulary words (e.g., *circular, horizontal*).	Extend learning by asking children what about the music made them move their body in a certain way.

End: Give children a warning just before you play the last music selection. To transition to the next activity, challenge children to move three body parts at the same time.

Follow-up: As you play with the children outside, wonder how they could use a part or parts of their bodies in different ways on the same equipment and/or move from one location to another. At large-group time, continue to play various types of music — especially music from different cultures — and challenge children to explore moving their bodies to the qualities of the music.

9 Keeping Balloons in the Air

Summary description: Children use their bodies to keep balloons in the air.

Time of day: Large-group time

Materials:

♦ Inflated balloons (do not use helium), one per person plus several extras

♦ Paper plates or pool noodles as backup materials for hitting balloons

Curriculum content: KDI 42. Movement. *Also:* KDI 35. Spatial awareness

COR Advantage item: Z. Movement. *Also:* item T. Geometry: Shapes and spatial awareness

Beginning: Show the balloons to the children and say that today the challenge is for each child to keep his or her balloon in the air. To demonstrate, keep your balloon in the air by hitting it from underneath with your hand. Give each child a balloon, help the children spread out (to minimize their bumping into each other), and say something like "I wonder how you will keep your balloons in the air."

Middle: Ask children what parts of their bodies other than their hands they can use to keep their balloons in the air (for example, heads, shoulders, or feet). Describe — and encourage children to describe — what they are doing. Try out their ideas and encourage them to observe and try out one another's ideas. Midway through the activity, bring out backup materials for children to explore.

The chart at right offers an example, at each developmental level, of what children may say and do, along with ideas for scaffolding (supporting and gently extending) children's learning. For additional ideas, refer to the scaffolding chart for Movement on page 34. To read more about scaffolding, see page 20.

Scaffolding Learning at Each Developmental Level

Earlier	Middle	Later
Children may	***Children may***	***Children may***
Use both hands to keep their balloons in the air.	Use different parts of their bodies to keep balloons in the air.	Experiment with using different objects to keep the balloons afloat.
Adults can	***Adults can***	***Adults can***
Label (name) and imitate children's actions, naming body parts and using position and direction words: "You're getting both hands under the balloon and hitting it up in the air." Extend learning by suggesting children try using one hand at a time, or getting beneath the balloon and using their heads to keep it in the air.	Ask children to describe what they are doing so adults can try to do it too. Extend learning by introducing new vocabulary words and phrases such as *afloat, airborne, sailing through the air, sinking down, overhead, boost*, and *loft*.	Use the same backup materials that children are using and ask children what else they could try. Extend learning by suggesting children work with a partner and take turns keeping one balloon in the air, and by challenging the pairs to try keeping two balloons in the air at once.

End: Give children a two-minute warning before it's time to end the activity. Together, corral the balloons (e.g., in a net or large carton). Tell children to move like a balloon to the next activity in the routine.

Follow-up: Let children explore moving balloons in different ways with different objects — for example, moving them across the room (instead of up in the air) or moving them using (unsharp) kitchen utensils. On days when it is not too windy, bring balloons outside for children to play with.

10   *Body Opposites*

> **Summary description:** Children explore the concept of "opposites" with body movements.

Time of day: Large-group time

Materials:

None

Curriculum content: KDI 42. Movement. *Also:* KDI 46. Classifying

COR Advantage item: Z. Movement. *Also:* item BB. Observing and classifying

Beginning: Once children have the concept of opposites, remind them of familiar examples, such as a door that can be open or shut. Say something like "We can do opposite things with our bodies too." Open and shut your hands, then ask "What else on our body can we open and shut?" Acknowledge their ideas (eyes, arms, legs, mouth, ears, nose) and encourage children to try them.

Middle: Ask children for other opposite actions they can do with their body — for example, by moving up and down, bending and straightening, or reaching high and low. Encourage children to describe as well as demonstrate their ideas, and to observe and copy one another. Repeat their words and introduce new vocabulary words to describe their actions (such as *reverse*).

The chart at right offers an example, at each developmental level, of what children may say and do, along with ideas for scaffolding (supporting and gently extending) children's learning at each level. For additional ideas, refer to the scaffolding chart for Movement on page 34. To read more about scaffolding, see page 20.

Scaffolding Learning at Each Developmental Level

Earlier	Middle	Later
Children may	***Children may***	***Children may***
Create opposites using parts of their head and face.	Create opposites with their whole body; for example, by facing first forward and then backward.	Explore a variety of opposites using their own body and describe what they are doing.
Adults can	***Adults can***	***Adults can***
Copy and then label (name) children's actions: "You're opening and shutting your ears with your hands."	Use, and encourage children to use, position and direction words to describe their movements.	Use children's words (e.g., *high* and *low*, *up* and *down*) and introduce new terms (for example, *head first* and *butt first*, *arms straight* and *bent*, *legs outstretched* and *crooked*).
Extend learning by asking children what other parts of their faces they can use for doing opposite things: "What parts of your face can you open and shut without using your hands?"	Extend learning by asking children what other opposite things they can do with their whole body, including multiple ways to create the same opposite effect — for example, if a child demonstrates an opposite by first standing and then lying down on the floor, asking "How else could you make your body go high and low?" (for example, raising up on tiptoe and then crouching).	Extend learning by suggesting children work in pairs to do and describe opposite things with their body; for example, with one child facing the front of the room while the other faces the rear.

End: Ask children to create one more opposite and share it with the rest of the class. Tell children you'd like them to work in pairs to create opposites as they move to the next activity.

Follow-up: At times when children are actively moving (e.g., large-group time or outside time), now and then ask how they could do an opposite action; for example, pedaling forward and backward, or filling and emptying. When doing finger plays (such as "Open, Shut Them" or "The Eensy Weensy Spider"), ask children how they could "reverse" an action or create a new pair of opposites.

Activities for

Dramatic Play

When all is said and done, education is about preparation for effective living. In this context, we can see why teachers include dramatic activities in their instructional repertoires. Dramatic conventions offer a safe harbor for trying out the situations of life; for experimenting with expression and communication; and for deepening human understanding. (Catterall, 2002b, p. 69)

The Development of Dramatic Play in Children

Pretend play begins at about 18 months, as children imitate the actions and sounds of familiar people, animals, objects, and situations. Toddlers' pretend play is *solitary*, self-directed, and quite simple, for example, pretending to drink from a cup (Copple & Bredekamp, 2009). *Parallel* play (playing alongside others) appears in the second year, and becomes *social* or interactive (playing with others) at around age three. Preschoolers are increasingly able to enter into mature sociodramatic play, which involves agreeing on the topic, taking on complex roles, and sustaining the play with others over an extended period of time (Bodrova & Leong, 2007). Preschoolers' representational abilities allow their pretend play to become more sophisticated and imaginative (Kavanaugh, 2006), with fanciful scenes, coordinated roles, and complex story lines. However, without explicit adult support to extend these

scenarios, many four- and five-year-olds repeat the same sequences and actions with little variation (Bodrova & Leong, 2005).

The creation and use of props also becomes more flexible and detailed during preschool, often taking up more time than acting out the play scenario itself. In addition, children develop explicit rules for what each role entails (Leong & Bodrova, 2012). Preschoolers coordinate their actions with those of their play partners and correct one another if an action does not match the role or the agreed-upon story line (for example, if the customer pretends to serve pie to the waitress).

By late preschool, children are aware when they are acting out imaginary roles (Sobel, 2006). This knowledge helps them use dramatic play to work through their anxieties (Friedman, 2010). Yet their play often involves magical thinking and animism. They give lifelike qualities to inanimate objects, believing, for example, that goblins are real (Rosengren & Hickling, 2000), or that a roaring monster lives inside the vacuum cleaner (Gelman & Opfer, 2002). On the other hand, they know that walking through a wall isn't possible and either insist that the play adhere to the rules of physics or repeatedly emphasize that something is "make believe" (Subbotsky, 2004).

Like the other creative arts, sociodramatic play builds multiple skills, including language and literacy, numeracy, and emotional self-regulation. It is also significantly linked to later school achievement (Prairie, 2013; Rubin, Bukowski, & Parker, 2006). Exploring character helps children understand and articulate emotions, while sustaining the narrative thread in a play scenario develops sequential and abstract reasoning (Wanerman, 2010). Perhaps the strongest evidence for the attraction and benefits of social pretend play is that, compared to other types of play, children's interactions last longer, their levels of involvement are higher, larger numbers of children are drawn in, and children show more cooperation (Creasey, Jarvis, & Berk, 1998).

Materials and Equipment That Support Dramatic Play

Preschoolers' sociodramatic play is facilitated by the following types of materials and equipment:

- Blocks of all shapes, sizes, and materials (wood, cardboard, rubber)

- Small vehicles (cars, construction, farm, planes, boats, trains, buses)

- Large vehicles for outdoor play (wagon, bus, trailer attached to tricyles)

- Sheets, blankets, tarps, tents

- Dress-up clothes (male and female), including uniforms and equipment

- Tools and toolboxes; safety equipment (helmets, goggles)
- Multiracial dolls and puppets
- Baby equipment (bottles, rattles, blankets, stroller, carriage)
- Dollhouse, dollhouse people and furniture
- Little people (cloth, wooden, rubber, or plastic figures)
- Animals (cloth, wooden, rubber, plastic)
- Wooden village, city, and farm sets
- Steering wheel
- Child-size appliances and furniture
- Adult-size cooking and eating utensils
- Empty food containers; small items to use as pretend food (pebbles, leaves, shells)
- Cleaning equipment (broom and dustpan, sponges)
- Telephones (push button; smart phones with batteries removed)
- Characters for reenacting stories (commercially available or homemade)

For additional ideas, see *The HighScope Preschool Curriculum* (Epstein & Hohmann, 2012, Chapter 6, pp. 171–221).

Teaching Strategies That Support Dramatic Play

To encourage children's emerging capacity for sociodramatic play, try these teaching strategies during the program day:

Support children as they imitate what they see and hear.

As children imitate familiar people, objects, and events in their lives (a baby crying, a fire truck speeding, going to the doctor), comment on and imitate their actions. At recall time, encourage children to represent what they did or used at work time (for example, pretending to turn the pages of a book). Have them act out events on a field trip, such as riding on the bus, petting the animals, or eating at a picnic table.

Watch for and support imaginative role play throughout the classroom.

Provide ample space and materials for role play in all parts of the room. Large open areas inspire pretend play because they can be turned into whatever the children dream up — a castle, an island, or a campground. Encourage children to make their own props and supply the materials and tools they need to do so, such as wood and fabric scraps, rolls of paper, and all kinds of fasteners. Field trips and visitors also expand the range of children's dramatic play. In fact, new materials and experiences of all types inspire children to use their imagination and incorporate their ideas into pretend play.

Participate as a partner in children's pretend play.

Partnering in children's play must be done with sensitivity so the adult does not take over. Teachers should observe until there is a natural opening (for example, the children need someone to be the baby) and/or children explicitly invite the adult into the play scenario ("You be the monster"). Either way, the direction of the play should remain in the children's control. If adults do occasionally suggest an idea ("Suppose the monster is hungry"), they should respect the children's choice of whether to include it or drop it.

For more information on teaching strategies that support dramatic play in preschool, see Epstein (2012, Chapter 6).

Incorporating Cultural Diversity in Dramatic Play

Young children are exposed to many media images of people carrying out real or fantasy actions in actual and imaginary settings. Most often these reflect mainstream culture, which does not necessarily look or sound like their own experiences. Children benefit from knowing that the people and events that make up their lives can also be depicted in dramatic representations. Ask families if there are particular personalities or formats representing their cultures that are popular at home. Preschoolers also use dramatic play to reenact their own daily experiences, as well as to explore the world of make believe and "what if." To enable their creativity, provide children with props, puppets, and story ideas they can use to elaborate and extend their pretend play. Here are some suggestions to widen the world of dramatic play that young children encounter and create.

Artists (playwrights, directors, performers, production designers). You might talk about and show examples of work by the following artists: Langston Hughes (African-American playwright); Zora Neale Hurston (African-American playwright); August Wilson (African-American playwright); Anna Deavere Smith (African-American playwright, actress); Glynn Washington (African American storyteller); Spike Lee (African-American film director); Amma Asante (African-American film director); Denzel Washington (African-American actor); Halle Berry (African-American actress); Wynn Thomas (African-American production designer); John Leguizamo (Hispanic actor, playwright); Edward James Olmos (Hispanic actor); Benicio Del Toro

(Hispanic actor); Gael Garcia Bernal (Hispanic actor); Rita Moreno (Hispanic actress); Penelope Cruz (Hispanic actress); Guillermo del Toro (Hispanic film director); Randy Barcello (Hispanic set and costume designer); Yussef El Guindi (Arab-American playwright); Kathy Najimy (Arab-American actress); Tony Shalhoub (Arab-American actor); Ang Lee (Asian-American film director); Margaret Cho (Asian-American actress); Lucy Liu (Asian-American actress); George Takei (Asian-American actor); Lynn Riggs (Native American playwright); Will Rogers (Native American actor and film producer); Jay Silverheels (Native American actor).

Genres. The following are genres you could introduce children to, which together reflect a diversity of cultures and influences: Noh and Kabuki drama (Japan); pantomime; storytelling (Brazil, China, Korea, Russia, Tibet, Native American cultures); Akan oral tradition (Ghanaian storytelling and music); Autos Sacramentales (Spanish religious dramas); Sanskrit drama (India); Bunraku (Japanese puppet theater); Yoruba theater (Nigeria); Kathakali (Indian dance drama); Ta'Zieh (Muslim passion plays); Trickster (Native American story and drama shape-shifting character).

Materials. You could introduce children to the following materials, which reflect and teach about a diversity of cultures: household items from different cultures (e.g., clothing, cooking utensils, and empty food containers); storybooks and informational books about people, landscapes, work roles, and activities in other countries; puppets and marionettes with diverse faces and costumes; playbills and performance posters of theater productions featuring other places and eras.

Adapting Dramatic Play Materials and Activities for Children With Special Needs

To offer all children the opportunity to engage in dramatic play activities, consider the following suggestions:

- Provide a wide diversity of pretend play props that offer visual, auditory, olfactory, and tactile choices (e.g., dress-up clothes with bells on them; spice jars in the house area).

- Use grips, tape, and straps so children can manipulate pretend play props and tools.

- Encourage children to represent objects and actions according to their capabilities (e.g., to make a firefighter's hat and/or move like a fire truck and/or to make a siren sound).

Adapting Dramatic Play Materials and Activities for Children Who Are Dual Language Learners (DLLs)

Consider the following strategies for supporting children for whom English is their second language:

- Encourage children to name and describe, in their home language, the props and actions they use in their pretend play scenarios, and provide the English equivalent.

- Label pretend play equipment and materials in the language(s) children in the classroom speak, as well as in English.

- Encourage DLL children and native English speakers to collaborate during dramatic play activities, sharing their discoveries and ideas, and helping one another solve problems.

- Use "action dialogues" with DLL children (communicating with gestures, rather than words) during pretend play scenarios. Occasionally introduce the English words for these actions.

- Partner DLLs with native English speakers during pretend play activities. Act as a translator to help children understand and carry out one another's ideas. Check with DLL children to make sure you have correctly understood and communicated their ideas. Check with native English speakers to make sure they understand the DLL children's intentions.

1 Acting Out Nursery Rhymes

Summary description: Children act out a familiar nursery rhyme, using facial expressions, gestures, whole body movements, and props.

Time of day: Large-group time

Materials:

♦ None initially, but add props appropriate to the rhyme as backup materials. For example, for "Mary Had a Little Lamb," add a crook (cane) for Mary and a bell for the "lamb" to wear around his or her neck

♦ Optionally, a nursery rhyme book with an illustration for "Mary Had a Little Lamb"

Curriculum content: KDI 43. Pretend Play. *Also:* KDI 24. Phonological awareness

COR Advantage item: AA. Pretend Play. *Also:* item N. Phonological awareness

Beginning: Recite "Mary Had a Little Lamb." Repeat the rhyme together with the children. Then say something like "Today we're going to act out the story in the rhyme." Ask for volunteers. To minimize waiting, have one child pretend to be Mary while several children pretend to be the lambs who follow her around. The other children can recite the rhyme as the volunteers act it out.

Middle: Have children take turns and switch roles. Encourage them to use facial expressions, gestures, and whole-body movements to express what the characters do, think, and feel. For example, you might ask, "What did the littlest lamb do? The biggest lamb?" Or you might say, "I wonder what else Mary could do while the lambs follow her." Midway through the activity, offer the props and ask children to suggest others.

The chart at right offers an example, at each developmental level, of what children may say and do, along with ideas for scaffolding (supporting and gently extending) children's learning at each level. For additional ideas, refer to the scaffolding chart for Pretend Play on page 35. To read more about scaffolding, see page 20.

Scaffolding Learning at Each Developmental Level

Earlier	Middle	Later
Children may	**Children may**	**Children may**
Move in ways consistent with the rhyme (e.g., look behind themselves when they walk, take steps as long or short as the child playing Mary).	Use facial expressions and gestures to act out their parts.	Incorporate props to act out the rhyme.
Adults can	**Adults can**	**Adults can**
Comment on children's actions: "You're looking behind you to make sure the lambs are following." Extend learning by asking children what else the character in the rhyme might do; for example, "How else could Mary lead the lambs around?"	Label and describe what children do: "You're shaking your head because two of the lambs aren't following you." Extend learning by encouraging children to describe their actions and expressions to the group, and suggesting children elaborate on one another's ideas: "Rene is skipping — how else could she move so the lambs will follow and do the same thing?"	Comment on how children use props "Stevie used a broom for a shepherd's crook; here's a bell for the lamb — I wonder how you could attach it." Extend learning by encouraging children to choose or make additional props (optionally, look at an illustration with the children as a source of additional ideas) — for example, "What does Mary wear when she leads the lambs around? I wonder what we could use from the dress-up area."

End: When it's time to finish up, tell children there will be one more reenactment. Have them move to the next daily routine activity in pairs, with one child being Mary and the other following like the lamb.

Follow-up: Repeat this activity with other familiar nursery rhymes or poems such as "Little Miss Muffet." Ask children to suggest their favorites. (Also see the activity "Mime the Rhyme on p. 144.")

2

Recipe for Fun

Summary description: Children "write" and illustrate recipes of their own creation.

Time of day: Small-group time

Materials:

♦ Cooking utensils (pots and pans, spoons, spatulas, sieves, measuring cups and spoons, plates and bowls, silverware and so on)

♦ Cookbooks and sample recipe cards

♦ Blank index cards

♦ Writing and drawing materials (crayons, colored pencils, markers)

Curriculum content: KDI 43. Pretend Play. *Also:* KDI 29. Writing and KDI 36. Measuring

COR Advantage item: AA. Pretend Play. *Also:* item R. Writing and item U. Measurement

Beginning: Talk with the children about helping their families cook at home or pretending to cook in the house area. Say that sometimes when we cook, we follow a recipe that tells us what ingredients to mix together and how to cook them. Let them look through the cookbooks and sample recipe cards. Give each child some cooking utensils, a recipe card, and a blank card with writing materials. Say something like "Today we're going to cook and write down our own recipes."

Middle: Talk with the children about what they are cooking, the types of food they enjoy eating, and whether they are including those ingredients in their recipes. Describe their actions as they cook (chopping, slicing, stirring, baking, frying). Encourage children to "write" or "draw" their recipes at whatever level they are able; take dictation when children request it.

The chart at right offers an example, at each developmental level, of what children may say and do, along with ideas for scaffolding (supporting and gently extending) children's learning. For additional ideas, refer to the scaffolding chart for Pretend Play on page 35. To read more about scaffolding, see page 20.

Scaffolding Learning at Each Developmental Level

Earlier	Middle	Later
Children may	***Children may***	***Children may***
Pretend to cook, using a variety of utensils.	Give a familiar name to their recipe, such as "macaroni and cheese," and may attempt to write letters and/or words on the cards.	Invent a unique name for their recipe, such as "monster pizza" or "Lego pie," and/or write or dictate a list of ingredients and draw a representational picture.
Adults can	***Adults can***	***Adults can***
Imitate and label children's actions, using familiar words (such as *frying*) and occasionally introducing new ones (such as *sauteeing*); pretend to eat what children make. Extend learning by asking children what they are cooking, what ingredients they are using, and how they will cook the food.	Answer children's questions about how to write letters or spell words. Extend learning by asking children what other ingredients they could add, what utensils are needed, how long it will take to cook their dish, and so on.	Ask children to "read" their recipe and describe their picture. Extend learning by asking children "how much" of each ingredient they need, using the measuring tools to help them indicate relative amounts, and by asking them to give instructions on how to combine and cook the ingredients.

End: Together with the children, put away the cooking utensils and put the recipe cards in a box in the house area. Tell children to move like spaghetti (or another favorite food) to the next activity in the daily routine.

Follow-up: As children play in the house area, talk with them about the foods they pretend to cook and serve. Ask families to bring in empty food containers and cooking utensils unique to their cuisines (such as a wok or tortilla press). At snacktime, ask children how they think the foods they are eating are made. Take a field trip to a restaurant to observe cooks at work. (Check with restaurant staff beforehand about kitchen safety and health department regulations.)

3

Blast Off

> **Summary description:** Building upon an ongoing interest (such as rockets), children invent and act out a story.

Time of day: Large-group time

Materials:

♦ Carpet squares (one per person)
♦ For backup, props related to the play theme (for example, helmets, hoses, padded vests)

Curriculum content: KDI 43. Pretend Play. *Also:* KDI 16. Gross-motor skills and KDI 21. Comprehension

COR Advantage item: AA. Pretend Play. *Also:* item I. Gross-motor skills and item M. Listening and comprehension

Beginning: Pick a theme that children incorporate into their play, but one that they need help extending and expanding upon (such as making rockets and blasting off into space). Begin with a story; for example:

Teacher: Today we're going on a mission to outer space. Where should we land our rocket ship?

Children: Mars!

Teacher: Okay, our mission is headed to Mars. Please get into your rocket ship and buckle up for safety. (Step on a carpet square and pretend to buckle up. Have the children do this as well.)

Teacher: I wonder what we need to do to start this rocket ship.

Children: Turn the key (push the buttons; count down; blast off).

Middle: Ask children how to act out those ideas, then follow their suggestions. Pretend to fly through space and encounter other celestial bodies; for example, you might say, "Oh no, an asteroid is headed straight for us. How can we dodge it?" Pretend to land and walk on Mars, then ask children what they need to stay safe there (e.g., helmet, space suit) and what they might find (e.g., rocks, aliens).

The chart at right offers an example, at each developmental level, of what children may say and do, along with ideas for scaffolding (supporting and gently extending) children's learning at each level. For additional ideas, refer to the scaffolding chart for Pretend Play on page 35. To read more about scaffolding, see page 20.

Scaffolding Learning at Each Developmental Level

Earlier	Middle	Later
Children may	***Children may***	***Children may***
Act out the ideas of others but not contribute their own.	Contribute one or two ideas/actions based on familiar themes, such as jumping up to indicate "take off" or falling down to represent a "crash landing."	Contribute many ideas that elaborate on the original story; for example, running out of fuel and landing on a planet other than Mars.
Adults can	***Adults can***	***Adults can***
Describe and label children's actions; for example, by saying something like "You're pulling the seatbelt really tight." Extend learning by asking children how else they might do something or what else they might see: "Suppose it's really cold on Mars — how would you walk then?" or "Do you suppose there are other space creatures on Mars? What would they sound like? How would they move?"	Call the attention of children to other children's ideas and encourage everyone to carry them out: "Daryl says to float in space." Extend learning by introducing new words such as *accelerate* or *impact* and explaining the words using terms the children already know — for example, "*Accelerate* means to go faster and faster."	Continue to ask what might happen next and follow children's ideas. Extend learning by encouraging children to provide more details for their suggestions: "How do the aliens move? What do they wear (or eat, etc.)? What games do alien children play?"

End: Tell the children it is time to get back in the rocket ship, buckle up, and head home. After you land, put the carpet squares away. Ask the children to travel through space a different way as they journey to the next activity in the daily routine.

Follow-up: Create similar story starters using other means of transportation that appear in the children's play themes, such as cars, buses, trains, or boats. Children can also act out their ideas using puppets, dolls, or small action figures.

4   *Storybook Drama*

Summary description: Children act out a favorite book such as *Where the Wild Things Are,* by Maurice Sendak.

Time of day: Large-group time

Materials:

None initially but, as backup, you could include props such as Max's wand and crown, and the dinner (use a bowl and spoon) his mother left

Curriculum content: KDI 43. Pretend play. *Also:* KDI 21. Comprehension

COR Advantage item: AA. Pretend Play. *Also:* item M. Listening and comprehension

Beginning: (*Note:* To make sure children are familiar with *Where the Wild Things Are,* by Maurice Sendak, read it several times in the week preceding this activity.) Tell the children that today they are going to act out the book *Where the Wild Things Are*. Help them recall how it starts by saying something like "What did Max do the night he wore his wolf suit?" Solicit suggestions on ways to show how Max "made mischief of one kind and another" and act out their ideas. Welcome all children's suggestions. Then say something like "Let's act out your ideas. Here are some props we can use."

Middle: Continue to help children recall the sequence of events in the book and invite their ideas on ways to act them out. Ask questions such as "What happens next?" or "How does Max feel when they make him king of all the wild things? How can we show that?" Encourage children to use the props if they are interested.

The chart at right offers an example, at each developmental level, of what children may say and do, along with ideas for scaffolding (supporting and gently extending) children's learning at each developmental level. For additional ideas, refer to the scaffolding chart for Pretend Play on page 35. To read more about scaffolding, see page 20.

Scaffolding Learning at Each Developmental Level

Earlier	Middle	Later
Children may	***Children may***	***Children may***
Follow the lead of others; for example, they may stomp their feet like a wild thing or wave an imaginary wand in the air.	Recall several events and suggest ways to dramatize them, such as Max's mother getting angry or Max finding his dinner waiting when he returns home.	Recall most of the events in the book, in sequence; talk in the voice of different characters, such as Max's mother or a wild thing; use props to act out actual or additional scenes, such as beads to stand for wild berries that Max gathers in the forest; interact with one or two others to carry out their ideas.
Adults can	***Adults can***	***Adults can***
Describe and imitate children's actions. Extend learning by providing prompts to help children remember and act out what happens: "How could you show how Max got to where the wild things live?"	Comment on those scenes and wonder how Max felt when they happened: "How could you show Max was sad?" Extend learning by asking for directions on how to act out children's ideas: "What should I do to show his mother is being angry at Max?"	Partner in children's play, taking on the role(s) children assign to them. Extend learning by inviting children to imagine scenarios that go beyond the book — "Suppose Max went to another faraway place; where do you think he might go?" — and encouraging children to create scenarios together.

End: Finish with Max returning home to find his hot dinner waiting. Together with the children, put the props away. Tell them to pretend they are on a sailboat as they travel to the next activity.

Follow-up: Reenact other familiar books, such *Goodnight Gorilla,* by Peggy Rathmann. Ask children to imagine what happens after a story ends; for example, you might say, "After Max eats dinner, what does he do?" or "What happens when the zookeeper wakes up the next morning?"

5   *Animal Singing*

Summary description: Children sing a familiar song while pretending to be different animals.

Time of day: Large-group time

Materials:

Bag containing pictures or figures of two or three animals (e.g., bear, lion, dog, bird, cat, dinosaur)

Curriculum content: KDI 43. Pretend play. *Also:* KDI 9. Emotions and KDI 41. Music

COR Advantage item: AA. Pretend play. *Also:* item D. Emotions and item Y. Music

Beginning: Together with the children, sing a simple song they know and like, such as "Twinkle, Twinkle, Little Star." Pick an animal out of the bag and say, for example, "I wonder how a lion would sing that song." Try out a few suggestions, saying something like "Rona says a lion would sing it loud. Let's try that" or "Franco says it would chomp its teeth. Let's sing and chomp our teeth at the same time."

Middle: After using the animals in the bag, have children suggest other animals and ways to sing as if they were those animals. Describe, and encourage children to describe, how they vary their voice. For example, you might say, "You're singing high and squeaky like a mouse" or "Theo is singing growly like a bear."

The chart at right offers an example, at each developmental level, of what children may say and do, along with ideas for scaffolding (supporting and gently extending) children's learning at each level. For additional ideas, refer to the scaffolding chart for Pretend Play on page 35. To read more about scaffolding, see page 20.

Scaffolding Learning at Each Developmental Level

Earlier	Middle	Later
Children may	**Children may**	**Children may**
Make animal sounds without singing the song.	Alter their voice in a limited number of ways, using a couple of variations for several different animals.	Use many vocal variations to represent different animals and suggest animals other than those in the bag.
Adults can	**Adults can**	**Adults can**
Describe and imitate children's sounds, including without singing; for example, "We're barking like dogs." Extend learning by saying "I'm going to try *singing* the song in that same soft (or loud, high-pitched, etc.) voice," then singing the song and encouraging the children to sing along, while accepting children's choice if they don't sing.	Suggest children listen to and imitate one another: "I wonder if you can make your voice roar like José's — he's pretending to be a lion." Extend learning by wondering how else each animal might sing the song: "You sang loud when you were pretending to be a lion; how would a dog singing the song sound different from a lion?"	Describe all the different ways the children are using their voice: "You sang high when you were a bird and way down low when you were a hippopotamus." Extend learning by challenging children to sing like the same animal but under different circumstances — such as a hungry lion and a tired lion, or a happy mouse and a frustrated mouse — commenting on the differences in their voice.

End: Warn children before introducing the last animal. Put your fingers to your lips and tell children to move "silently" like that animal to the next activity.

Follow-up: Repeat this activity with different songs, encouraging children to suggest their favorites. Try having children sing the same song as an animal experiencing different feelings or situations. Children might also choose to move as well as sing to represent each animal.

6

We're Workers Too

> **Summary description:** After a field trip to a work site, such as a produce stand, children pretend to carry out the roles they observed.

Time of day: Small-group time, following a field trip

Materials:

- Open-ended materials to represent fruits, vegetables, and flowers (such as balls, blocks, beads, pegs, pipe cleaners)
- Baskets or other containers with handles
- Props brought back from the field trip (such as adhesive labels, berry baskets)
- Materials and tools to make additional props, such as paper money, charge-card readers

Curriculum content: KDI 43. Pretend play. *Also:* KDI 53. Diversity and KDI 54. Community roles

COR Advantage item: AA. Pretend play. *Also:* item FF. Knowledge of self and others

Beginning: Take a field trip to a nearby workplace, such as a produce stand, where people unload and arrange fruits, vegetables, and flowers. Talk with staff beforehand about what is likely to interest the children, and discuss safety concerns. Take photos. At small-group time the next day, recall the trip with the children. Focus on one part, such as stacking the produce. Give each child a basket of materials and say something like "I wonder how you'll arrange your vegetables, fruits, and flowers."

Middle: Encourage children to describe the materials and how they use them. Help them connect what they are doing to what they saw on the field trip. Encourage them to solve problems, such as keeping balls ("apples") from rolling off the table. Converse with children about when and where they buy produce with their own families. Encourage them to use the additional materials and props on the table.

The chart at right offers an example, at each developmental level, of what children may say and do, along with ideas for scaffolding (supporting and gently extending) children's learning at each level. For additional ideas, see the scaffolding chart for Pretend Play on page 35. To read more about scaffolding, see page 20.

Scaffolding Learning at Each Developmental Level

Earlier	Middle	Later
Children may	***Children may***	***Children may***
Play with the materials but not relate them to the field trip.	Reenact one or two events, such as piling the "tomatoes" or gathering pipe cleaners into a "bunch of flowers."	Pretend by using many props and actions. such as stacking "oranges," filling baskets, and selling to customers.
Adults can	***Adults can***	***Adults can***
Label and imitate children's actions: "You're lining up all the pegs." Extend learning by looking at the pictures and then using materials in the ways depicted in the photos — (e.g., putting beads in a berry basket); watch for children to join in, while respecting their choice if they don't.	Narrate children's actions and how they relate to what happened at the market. Extend learning by inviting children to recall other details: "Help me remember what the woman did after she sprayed water on the broccoli."	Share memories of the trip: "More people bought oranges than melons." Extend learning by encouraging children to make additional props, such as price stickers (helping as needed), and asking children how to show additional details: "How could we act out when the man carefully piled the peaches so they wouldn't get bruised?"

End: Give children a five-minute warning before the end of the activity, and then clean up together. Remind children of where they can find the materials if they want to use them at work (choice) time. Have them transition to the next activity in the routine using a motion they saw at the work site, such as carrying, lifting, or polishing.

Follow-up: Visit other workplaces of interest to the children (e.g., a pizza parlor, bakery, pet store, supermarket, library, garage, or train or truck loading dock). Recall the event the next day and provide relevant props for children to act out the roles they observed.

7 Mime the Rhyme

Summary description: Children fill in the last word of a couplet (a two-line poem) and then act out the rhyme using pantomime (body gestures and facial expressions only).

Time of day: Large-group time

Materials:
None (children use their own bodies)

Curriculum content: KDI 43. Pretend play. *Also:* KDI 24. Phonological awareness

COR Advantage item: AA. Pretend play. *Also:* item N. Phonological awareness

Beginning: Play a rhyming game with the children. Give them the first line, and the beginning of the second line, and have them add the final word or phrase. For example, say "As I was walking down the road, I saw a giant carrying a ____." Or "Yesterday I went to the fair, where I saw a ____." After each couplet, encourage children to act out the idea in pantomime; that is, by using body movements and gestures only — no words or sounds.

Middle: Continue to recite rhymes for children to fill in and mime. If they suggest ideas — for example, by saying something like "Do one about the circus" — turn them into couplets with the last word or phrase missing: "The circus clown said boo, and I went ____." Encourage children to add their own ideas and build on one another's suggestions, first filling in a rhyme and then miming it. Remind children not to use sounds or words for the miming parts, but accept their choice if they do."

The chart at right offers an example, at each developmental level, of what children may say and do, along with ideas for scaffolding (supporting and gently extending) children's learning at each level. For additional ideas, refer to the scaffolding chart for Pretend Play on page 35. To read more about scaffolding, see page 20.

Scaffolding Learning at Each Developmental Level

Earlier	Middle	Later
Children may	**Children may**	**Children may**
Fill in a nonrhyming word and/or copy the miming movements of their peers.	Fill in a rhyming word, either real (*toad*) or nonsense (*boad*); they will create simple mimes, but occasionally use sounds.	Suggest an idea or the first line of a couplet; create elaborated mimes using multiple gestures and facial expressions.
Adults can	**Adults can**	**Adults can**
Refrain from correcting children while repeating their words and encouraging others to copy their ideas. Extend learning by repeating the couplet and asking for a word that rhymes, giving an example, and also by encouraging children to mime the new rhyme.	Ask children to describe their ideas for the adults to carry out. Extend learning by wondering aloud how to act out a child's idea without sounds, and by asking children to suggest another word and/or mime to complete a couplet.	Copy children's actions and encourage their peers to do the same. Extend learning by introducing new vocabulary words for whole body movements (*somersaulting*), gestures (*flailing*), and facial expressions (*grimace*).

End: Let the children know when you are about to present the last couplet. Have them use the last action word of the couplet as a suggestion for moving to the next activity.

Follow-up: Create couplets based on children's interests that you observe at work (choice) and outside time: "I pretended I was a cat, and I made a ____" or "A worm dug in the sand, and he ate a ____." Encourage children to invent mimes for the rhyming words they invent; for example, you might say, 'Show us what a *glat* does" or "Should we make a yummy or yucky face when we eat *mand?*"

8   *Dressing Dolls*

Summary description: Children make up stories about where dolls will go and dress them accordingly.

Time of day: Small-group time

Materials:

- Small dolls or figures, undressed (such as flexible rubber dolls or wooden mannequins with jointed limbs, available online from art supply outlets)
- Fabric scraps
- Trim and accessories (such as ribbon, lace, mesh, small scarves, hair ties, and beaded bracelets)
- Pipe cleaners, tape, scissors

Curriculum content: KDI 43. Pretend play. *Also:* KDI 17. Fine-motor skills

COR Advantage item: AA. Pretend play. *Also:* item J. Fine-motor skills

Beginning: Tell the children that the dolls are getting ready to go somewhere and need to get dressed. Talk with children about where they think the dolls are going and what kind of clothes they need to wear. Give each child a doll and a small basket of the other materials.

Middle: Listen to and comment on the activities children create for the dolls, and how they dress them; for example, you might ask, "What will he wear to stay warm at the hockey game?" Explain how and why you dressed your doll, saying, for example, "She needs a hat at the beach to keep the sun out of her eyes." Encourage children to share the materials and to invent scenarios with two or more dolls.

The chart at right offers an example, at each developmental level, of what children may say and do, along with ideas for scaffolding (supporting and gently extending) children's learning at each level. For additional ideas, refer to the scaffolding chart for Pretend Play on page 35. To read more about scaffolding, see page 20.

Scaffolding Learning at Each Developmental Level

Earlier	Middle	Later
Children may	***Children may***	***Children may***
Explore ways to make the doll move and dress a doll — for example, wrapping it in a scarf — but not tell a story.	Name and dress their doll and create a simple story about where the doll will go: "She's going to play on the swings"; as children sometimes do with pretend play, they may spend more time creating props than acting out the scenario.	Create doll clothes with multiple materials and invent multistep stories; for example, "He's going to the store to buy cereal and milk, and then he's going to drive the fire truck to the mall and save all the babies."
Adults can	***Adults can***	***Adults can***
Say where the adult's doll is going and how it is dressed. Extend learning by encouraging children to add more items to a doll's outfit and by saying something like "Now your doll is all dressed — I wonder where he'll go."	Ask children to describe the materials and tools they used to make the doll's clothes. Extend learning by encouraging children to add details to their story: "What else will your doll do at the playground?"	Ask if the adult's doll can come along, and ask how to dress the doll to help the child's doll. Extend learning by encouraging children to collaborate on stories and to dress and use several dolls together to carry out their play scenarios.

End: Give children a three-minute warning before the end of the activity and then clean up together, reminding children where they can find the materials to use at work (choice) time. Tell the children to move like a doll bending its arms and legs as they transition to the next activity in the daily routine.

Follow-up: Repeat this activity with toy animals and other figures. Add dress-up clothes and accessories to the house area, inviting donations from families. During work (choice) time, talk about how children dress themselves, dolls, or other figures and how it fits their play scenarios. Become a partner in their play themes, dressing and acting according to the children's directions.

9

Farm Walk

Summary description: Children pretend to walk around a farm and make the motions and sounds of the things they see and hear.

Time of day: Large-group time

Materials:
None

Curriculum content: KDI 43. Pretend play. *Also:* KDI 22. Speaking

COR Advantage item: AA. Pretend play. *Also:* item L. Speaking

Beginning: Say something like "Today we're going for a walk around the farm." March in place. Then stop, point, and say "I see a cow." Go "Moo," get on your knees and pretend to eat grass. Encourage the children to imitate you. Then stand, start to march again, and say something like "I wonder what we'll see next on our walk around the farm." Pretend to be one more thing — for example, a tractor or another animal — and solicit the children's ideas for sounds and movements.

Middle: Each time you resume marching, ask each of the children, in turn, to suggest something they see and to give directions for how to act it out. Encourage children to use their imagination — that is, to not be bound by things actually in that place but to add things they make up, such as flying monsters or strange animals.

The chart at right offers an example, at each developmental level, of what children may say and do, along with ideas for scaffolding (supporting and gently extending) children's learning at each level. For additional ideas, refer to the scaffolding chart for Pretend Play on page 35. To read more about scaffolding, see page 20.

Scaffolding Learning at Each Developmental Level

Earlier	Middle	Later
Children may	**Children may**	**Children may**
Offer a familiar sound or sight, such as a duck quacking or a farmer putting seeds in the ground.	Suggest several sights and sounds typically encountered on a farm, including animals and machinery.	Add story elements that are not specific to a farm, such as walking down the road and encountering vehicles from outer space.
Adults can	**Adults can**	**Adults can**
Imitate children's sounds and actions. Extend learning by asking children what else they might see and how adults and the other children can act it out.	Describe what children are acting out and encourage children to describe it too: "How high should we reach for the berries? What should we do with the berries after we pick them off the bush?" Extend learning by challenging children to think of something that "surprises" them to discover on a farm.	Go along with the fantasy and encourage the other children to join in: "Brill says there's a big space station behind the barn; I wonder what sounds are coming from it?" Extend learning by probing for additional story elements and narrative details — for example, by asking questions like "What happens next? How should we act that out?"

End: Tell the children when it's time to return home, and ask for suggestions on what to look and listen for on the "walk" back. Have children move to the next activity in the routine like an animal or a machine they saw on the farm walk.

Follow-up: Use this idea for other walks, such as those down the street, through the woods, or in the park. Be sure to include places and situations appropriate to where you live (city, suburb, shore, mountains, or countryside). Have children imagine a walk through a place that is familiar from a favorite storybook; for example, you and the children might take a walk through the place "where the wild things are."

10   *Story Emotions*

Summary description: After the teacher tells a two-sentence story about a child experiencing an emotion, children talk about and act out that emotion.

Time of day: Large-group time

Materials:
None

Curriculum content: KDI 43. Pretend play. *Also:* KDI 9. Emotions

COR Advantage item: AA. Pretend play. *Also:* item D. Emotions

Beginning: Tell a brief (two sentence) story starter that involves an emotion; for example, "One day Keisha wanted to put together the animal puzzle. When she saw that the piece with the goat was missing, she got angry!" Ask the children, "What do you think Keisha did when she got angry?" Act out their ideas — saying, for example, "She stomped her foot!" or "She got a different puzzle."

Middle: Repeat the process with another story starter; for example, "Jackson's daddy told him Grandma Lacy was coming to dinner and bringing a special dessert. 'Wow!' said Jackson. I'm so excited!'" If a child isn't sure how to act something out, ask others for their ideas. Tell different story starters for other emotions.

The chart at right offers an example, at each developmental level, of what children may say and do, along with ideas for scaffolding (supporting and gently extending) children's learning at each level. For additional ideas, refer to the scaffolding chart for Pretend Play on page 35. To read more about scaffolding, see page 20.

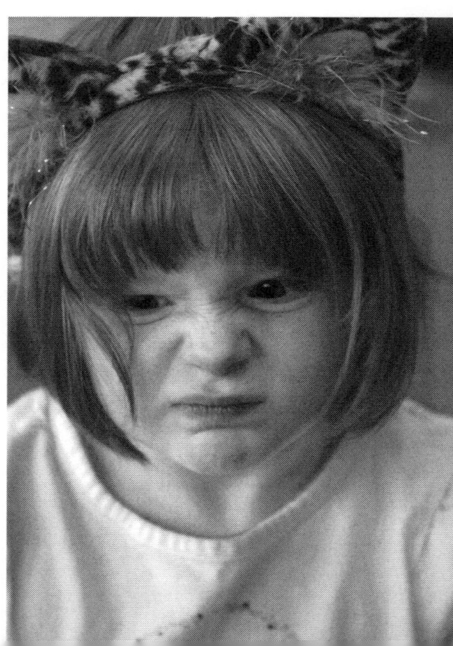

Scaffolding Learning at Each Developmental Level		
Earlier	**Middle**	**Later**
Children may	***Children may***	***Children may***
Suggest an emotion and a way to act it out.	Suggest emotions in addition to those in the story; for example, "She was *mad* and sad too!"	Add elements to the story starter; for example, "The horse was missing too. And the tiger!"
Adults can	***Adults can***	***Adults can***
Carry out children's ideas and encourage others to do the same; for example, "Latoya says to clap our hands to show we're happy." Extend learning by asking how else children could show that same emotion: "What else do you do when you feel happy?"	Talk about each emotion and ask for ways to act it out. Extend learning by asking children what other emotions they sometimes feel at the same time, and by soliciting ideas on how to show both emotions at once: "Just before bed, I sometimes feel tired and cranky at the same time— how can we show those feelings together?"	Act out these new elements, and ask questions like "How did Keisha feel when three animals in the puzzle were missing? How could we show she was really, really angry?" Extend learning by encouraging children to create their own story starters, with ways to act out how the characters are feeling: "Tell us about a time you were scared — how should we act that out?"

End: Tell children there will be one more story. Pick an emotion for which they have had many ideas and tell them to move to the next activity in the routine as if, for example, they are "really, really happy!"

Follow-up: As children engage in pretend play at work (choice) time, encourage them to act out the emotions in their play scenarios. For example, if a child says, "You're the mommy and you're scared because a robber is in the house," ask what to do to show you're scared. While reading books with the children, pause now and then to have them act out the emotions in the story.

Art Appreciation

(*Note:* The art appreciation activities are balanced among the four other creative arts areas. There are three each for visual art and music, and two each for movement and dramatic [pretend] play.)

The moral function of art itself is to remove prejudice, do away with the scales that keep the eye from seeing, tear away the veils due to wont and custom, perfect the power to perceive (John Dewey, 1934, p. 338).

The Development of Art Appreciation in Children

Research shows that young children are more capable of appreciating art than we give them credit for (Gardner, 1990). They are eager to share their reactions to a picture, song, dance, or story, provided the conversation springs from the features that interest them (Schiller, 1995). Preschoolers typically focus on the subject matter of the artwork, but they become aware of its qualitative aspects when adults call their attention to it. For example, they may notice whether a picture about a garden is set in sunshine or shadow, or whether the movements of a dancing bear are light or heavy. Likewise, preschoolers can categorize artwork based on perceptual qualities because of their natural interest in sorting things. For example, they can describe music as being smooth or jumpy, or characterize the mood of a short play as being funny or sad.

Young children can also reflect on what they see and hear, including what they think an artist is trying to say or how a work of art makes them feel. In simple terms, they can even say how they think the artwork

is affected by events in the artist's experience, such as who the artist knows, where the artist lives, or whether the artwork is set in the present or another time period. These are the same considerations that adults take into account when appreciating a work of art.

The cognitive and social-emotional development of preschoolers has implications for their ability to appreciate art in each of the media addressed in this book. For example:

- **Visual art —** Think of the learning environment as an art gallery in which children spend a large part of their day. Psychologist Bernard Spodek (2008) says, "There are many ways in which we can make children more sensitive to the beauty that surrounds them and help them understand the aesthetic elements in their culture. This requires that we surround the children with things that are beautiful and make the school setting more aesthetically pleasing" (p. 13).

- **Music —** The "magical thinking" of preschoolers may lead them to believe that music is created by the mechanical device emitting it instead of humans using their voices and/or playing instruments. It is therefore especially important for young children to hear live vocal and instrumental performances, which also develops their listening skills. The optimum concert length for preschoolers is 25 minutes. Where possible, allow children to touch the instruments (under supervision) and include time for them to ask the performers questions.

- **Dance —** Children understand the "language" of movement and get the emotions behind it, including humor and sadness (Friedman, 2010). Make performances participatory. It's difficult to sit still if others are moving about, so whether the dancing occurs in a studio or under the guidance of a visiting artist in the classroom, allow time and space for children to move too. Use preschoolers' emerging language skills to encourage them to describe their movements and the feelings they are expressing with their bodies. Also take advantage of their growing social awareness and sensitivity; moving together can be a community building event.

- **Theater —** Preschoolers are generally able to differentiate reality from fantasy, but it's a good idea to prepare them beforehand for any upsetting content and, if necessary, reassure them during the performance that it's only make-believe. As with books, it's okay to tackle scary or unsettling topics, as long as the ending is comforting. It's also important to make the performance participatory and to respect children's attention spans. Educators suggest 30–50 minutes for younger preschoolers and 60–75 minutes for older preschoolers (Friedman, 2010), but children vary widely. Begin with shorter experiences and lengthen them gradually.

In sum, appreciating art is well within the perceptual, cognitive, and social-emotional capacity of preschoolers. "Producing their own artwork is one of the ways in which children create meaning in their lives. But they can also discover meaning in the art created by others and in nature. Such discovery is what art appreciation is about. Art becomes a way of thinking about and perceiving the world [that] enriches human experience and creates new levels of understanding" (Epstein, 2005, p. 52).

Materials and Equipment That Support Art Appreciation

The materials listed below encourage young children to develop a sense of aesthetics, appreciate what artists do, and understand in general what the arts are all about.

- Books with different types of illustrations; for example, watercolor and oil paintings, simple and detailed line drawings, photographs, collages, realistic and abstract images

- Books written for children about artists (visual artists, musicians, dancers, actors, and other creative people); types (genres) of fine and performing arts; and making art in all genres

- Examples of visual art, music, and performing arts from children's homes and communities in all media including painting, drawing, sculpture, weaving, ceramics, woodwork; instrumental and vocal recordings; photographs of dances and dramatic performances; books about artists from different backgrounds; books written and illustrated by artists of different languages and cultures

- Postcards, posters, and brochures about art exhibits and performances

- Magazines and catalogs about museums, architecture, music, dance, and theatrical performances

- Displays of artwork by children

- Examples of artwork by fine and performing artists (reproductions, photographs, recordings, short videoclips) in different media and representing different genres

For additional ideas, see *The HighScope Preschool Curriculum* (Epstein & Hohmann, 2012, Chapter 6, pp. 171–221).

Teaching Strategies That Support Art Appreciation

Preschoolers will develop their ability to appreciate the creative arts when teachers regularly employ the strategies described below.

Focus on specific aspects of artwork when you explore it with children.

Begin with one aspect of an artwork (a bright color, a lovely sound, an unusual movement) that the children find particularly interesting. Encourage children to label and describe it. Gradually increase the complexity of the artwork as children are able to focus on more features. Describe, and help children describe, how the elements are related — for example, "The music got louder and faster at the same time" or "More children joined your 'pirate family' when you built a ramp for the boat."

Encourage children to make and explain simple aesthetic choices.

Making an artistic choice and saying why you do (or do not) like something takes knowledge and courage. To give children practice making aesthetic judgments, let them experience a wide variety of artistic styles so they can discover what appeals to them. Give them the "language" to talk about art. For example, talk about the lighting in a photograph or how they change their voices to play different characters. To help children feel comfortable expressing and explaining their choices, let them know that their opinions matter and will always be respected. Model this acceptance for others to follow.

Discuss the feelings expressed through artwork.

Children intuitively grasp what an artist is trying to express (for example, the music sounds "happy") before they are able to explain how this effect is achieved. Encourage children to talk about the feelings that artwork evokes in them, and to describe the elements they see or hear that bring about those feelings (for example, "The colors are dark. It looks scary"). When you display or send home artwork, talk with children and their parents about what the children were thinking or feeling when they created it.

Expose children to the materials, tools, and techniques used by artists.

Children typically see an artistic product with little awareness of the process behind its creation. Help them appreciate the varied materials, tools, and techniques that artists use. For example, display examples of embroidery or metalsmithing, as well as painting and sculpture. Bring in posters for concert, theater, and dance performances; mount them at children's eye level and encourage children to talk about them with parents at dropoff and pickup times. When possible, provide children with high-quality materials and tools to work with themselves. If you give them fine-pointed brushes, they will incorporate more detail in their own artwork. Encourage them to experiment in the same way artists do ("Seurat painted with many dots. I wonder what you could make that way").

Plan local field trips to introduce children to the creative arts.

Look for local arts venues — studios, galleries, performance spaces — that welcome young children. These include hands-on museums, fairs and festivals, landscaped parks, and art in public spaces. Visit a site before bringing the children, and talk to the people in charge to make sure they know how to actively engage preschoolers in the learning process. After the field trip, encourage children to represent their experiences. Ask artists to donate extra or scrap materials and "tools of the trade" for children to use on their own.

For more information on teaching strategies that support art appreciation in preschool, see Epstein (2012, Chapter 7).

Incorporating Cultural Diversity in Art Appreciation

In her *Young Children* interview with editor Derry Koralek (2010), arts educator Mimi Chenfeld says, "I think all children born into the human race should get a membership card that says they are entitled to the music, dance, stories, poems, and customs of their people" (p. 10). It is also important to expose preschoolers to the artists and arts experiences that lie outside their own families and communities. Children might otherwise not encounter this artistic diversity, but they will enjoy relating the images, sounds, movements, and ideas to their own lives. To diversify art appreciation in your classroom materials and daily activities, consider the following suggestions:

Artists — Include diverse artists and performers from around the world; from different racial, ethnic, cultural, and religious groups in this country; and from different geographical regions in this country.

Genres — Include artistic styles from around the world, and from different groups and regions in this country.

Materials — Include materials and tools representing varied media; visit the studios of artists from different backgrounds so children can observe how the materials and tools are used and (if feasible), use them themselves; bring materials and tools from artists' studios back to the classroom for the children to use.

For specific suggestions of artists and performers, genres, and materials in the areas of visual art, music, movement, and drama, see chapters 4–7, respectively.

Adapting Art Appreciation Materials and Activities for Children With Special Needs

To offer all children the opportunity to engage in art appreciation activities, consider the following suggestions:

- Provide books about artists and performers with disabilities (e.g., blind sculptor David Stephens; Wheelchair Dancers Organization; hearing-impaired percussionist Evelyn Glennie).

- Make sure museums, concert halls, theaters, and other field-trip destinations have handicapped access and facilities.

- Magnify and/or amplify, as appropriate, shared examples of artwork in all genres.

- Listen patiently as children express their aesthetic choices; accept different ways in which children indicate their artistic preferences (e.g., pointing, looking, moving toward, speaking).

Adapting Art Appreciation Materials and Activities for Children Who Are Dual Language Learners (DLLs)

Consider the following strategies for supporting children for whom English is their second language:

- Encourage children to describe, in their home language, works of art in all media and their aesthetic preferences, and provide the English equivalent.

- Label displays of artwork in the language(s) children in the classroom speak, as well as in English.

- Provide examples of artwork in various media with non-English titles and/or features, such as calligraphy, paintings and sculptures, song titles and words, dances and dance steps, and titles and characters in plays adapted for young children.

- Encourage DLL children and native English speakers to collaborate during art appreciation activities, sharing their discoveries and ideas, and helping one another solve problems.

- Partner DLLs with native English speakers during art appreciation activities. Act as a translator to help children understand and carry out one another's ideas. Check with DLL children to make sure you have correctly understood and communicated their ideas. Check with native English speakers to make sure they understand the DLL children's intentions.

1

How Artists Color Their Days

Summary description: After reading *My Many Colored Days,* by Dr. Seuss, children talk about how artists use colors to represent feelings and paint pictures to depict their own feelings.

Time of day: Small-group time

Materials:

♦ *My Many Colored Days,* by Dr. Seuss

♦ Paint (preferably in jars with pumps) in primary colors (red, yellow, blue), black, and white

♦ Cups (to hold paint), paper, paintbrushes

♦ Painting smocks

♦ Wet sponges, paper towels, bowls of water for cleanup (spread newspaper or plastic on the table to make cleanup easier)

Curriculum content: KDI 44. Appreciating the Arts. *Also:* KDI 40. Art, KDI 9. Emotions, and KDI 17. Fine-motor skills

COR Advantage item: X. Art. *Also:* item D. Emotions and item J. Fine-motor skills

Beginning: Read the book *My Many Colored Days,* by Dr. Seuss. Talk with children about why the author chose particular colors to represent his feelings. Make comments such as "I wonder what you would feel on a red (or other color) day?" Tell the class that today they are going to paint pictures about their day. Say "I wonder what colors you will use to show how you are feeling today." Distribute the paper, paintbrushes, and cups.

Middle: As you circulate, prompt children to remember things that happened that day and how they felt. For example, you might say something like "Yesterday it was raining too hard to go outside, but today is sunny. How does that make you feel?" or "You and Maria played cars at work time. I wonder what color would show how excited you were when your car went down the ramp really fast."

The chart at right offers an example, at each developmental level, of what children may say and do, along with ideas for scaffolding (supporting and gently extending) children's learning at each level. For additional ideas, refer to the scaffolding chart for Appreciating the Arts on page 36. To read more about scaffolding, see page 20.

Scaffolding Learning at Each Developmental Level

Earlier	Middle	Later
Children may	***Children may***	***Children may***
Explore using paints without relating them to feelings.	Say they chose a certain color because it is their "favorite" or make a remark unrelated to a feeling (such as "My bedroom is blue").	Talk about how a color reflects their feelings about an event that day: "I picked red because I was happy we had popcorn for snack."
Adults can	***Adults can***	***Adults can***
Label the color(s) children choose and comment on how they are using the paints: "You're using your fingers to make big circles with the blue paint." Extend learning by sharing the feelings one might associate with the color(s) children use; for example, "When I'm sad, yellow cheers me up."	Repeat children's comments and share a comparable observation (such as favorite colors). Extend learning by tying children's comments to feelings — for example, by asking how they feel when they wear their favorite color — or by talking with children about what they do in their room and how it makes them feel, such as when a parent reads to them at bedtime.	Acknowledge children's comments, saying something like "You like popcorn, and red is a happy color." Extend learning by asking children to imagine, and choose a color for, a different scenario: "Suppose we ate peanut butter crackers — what color would you choose then?"

End: Give children a five-minute warning before the end of the activity. Clean up together and remind the children where they can find the book and painting supplies. Have the children move to the next activity in the routine in a way that shows how they feel about the activity, such as happy, excited, or impatient.

Follow-up: As you read other familiar books with children, comment now and then on how the artist uses color to illustrate how the characters are feeling. (Be careful not to interrupt the flow of the story.) At message board time, ask how children feel about a new material or an upcoming event and what color you should use to write it on the board. At recall time, set out colored squares and ask children to choose the color that shows how they felt doing the activity they are recalling.

2 *Quilting With Fabric Squares*

Summary description: Children explore the aesthetic properties of different types of fabric as they create their own quilts.

Time of day: Small-group time

Materials:

- Photos of quilts (from art books, craft manuals, interior decorating magazines, postcards)
- Fabric pieces of different textures, colors, designs, and shapes (ask parents to bring in fabric scraps, particularly those that reflect materials and designs from other cultures)
- Colored masking tape
- Scissors

Curriculum content: KDI 44. Appreciating the Arts. *Also:* KDI 40. Art, KDI 17. Fine-motor skills, and KDI 38. Patterns

COR Advantage item: X. Art. *Also:* item J. Fine-motor skills and item V. Patterns

Beginning: Show children the pictures of quilts. Ask if they have quilts at home (e.g., bedspreads, pillows, potholders, wall hangings). Talk about how quilts are made "by stitching together different pieces of fabric to make a pattern or design." Pass around several samples of fabric for children to feel and look at, then give each child a basket with fabric scraps, tape, and scissors. Leave the rest in the middle of the table. Say something like "I wonder what the quilts you make will look like."

Middle: Talk with children about the colors, textures, and designs of the fabrics in their baskets. Comment on the fabrics they choose and how they arrange them; for example, you might say, "You're using lots of red and blue pieces in your quilt" or "The materials you chose feel soft." Encourage children to share and exchange samples and to explore the additional fabric scraps on the table. Help them with the tape or scissors as needed, and refer children to one another for assistance.

The chart at right offers an example, at each developmental level, of what children may say and do, along with ideas for scaffolding (supporting and gently extending) learning at each level. For additional ideas, refer to the scaffolding chart for Appreciating the Arts on page 36. To read more about scaffolding, see page 20.

Scaffolding Learning at Each Developmental Level

Earlier	Middle	Later
Children may	***Children may***	***Children may***
Choose single pieces of fabric and place tape all over them.	Choose fabric pieces at random but place them in a square or rectangle and may tape some or all of the pieces together, using one or more colors of tape.	Choose specific pieces of fabric or cut them to size to make a design they have in mind; they may express a preference for certain colors or patterns.
Adults can	***Adults can***	***Adults can***
Describe — and encourage children to describe — the characteristics of the material they are using, such as its color, width, or texture. Extend learning by comparing different pieces of cloth in children's baskets: "This piece is all one solid color; that one has lots of colors."	Comment on children's choices and how they arrange them: "You put all the light-colored pieces on the top and a row of dark fabric on the bottom; you attached them with red tape." Extend learning by looking at photos of quilts together and discussing how they are similar to and/or different from the arrangements the children are creating.	Encourage children to describe the materials and colored tape they are using and how they are piecing their quilts together. Extend learning by asking children why they chose a particular piece of fabric and/or color of tape, or why they particularly like something, as well as asking about the feelings evoked by the quilt's design: "You chose all bright colors. It reminds me of my flower garden."

End: Give children a five-minute cleanup warning. Children may choose to put the quilts in their cubbies to take home, or they may get a "work-in-progress" sign to express their intention to continue creating them at work (choice) time. Suggest to children that they move their arms and legs like scissors as they go to the next activity in the daily routine.

Follow-up: Incorporate a variety of fabrics into different areas of the room and outdoor play space (e.g., blankets in the house area; a patterned tarp over the sandbox). Ask families to bring in quilts for children to look at. Add more photos of quilts to the book area. Visit the remnant bin at a local fabric store. Take a field trip to an art gallery or craft fair that features quilts. Look at both the variety of materials and the types of stitching that quilters use.

3

Looking at Art Reproductions

Summary description: Children sort postcard reproductions of fine artwork based on their artistic (aesthetic) characteristics.

Time of day: Small-group time

Materials:

Reproductions of fine artwork (postcards from museum gift shops, or photos from art, craft, and architecture magazines that you cut out and make "postcards" out of), including paintings, sculpture, photography, prints, woodcuts, weaving, ceramics, and other media

Curriculum content: KDI 44. Appreciating the Arts. *Also:* KDI 40. Art, KDI 45. Observing, and KDI 46. Classifying

COR Advantage item: X. Art. *Also:* item BB. Observing and classifying

Beginning: Look at and discuss four cards with the children, pointing out such things as subject matter, medium, and the use of color, light, line, and so on. With input from the children, sort the cards into two piles (for example, one in which the artist used a lot of color and another in which the images are black and white; or two-dimensional and three-dimensional artwork). Give each child a set of four to six cards and say something like "I wonder what you will see in these artworks and how you will sort your cards."

Middle: Converse with children about the properties of the artwork on their cards. Describe and encourage them to describe features of interest to them, and how they include them in their own artwork. For example, you might say, "What colors do you use when you draw?" or "Sometimes you paint on a flat surface, and sometimes you build things that stand in the air." Introduce children to the vocabulary of art, using words such as *background, medium, color, line,* and *form.* Midway, add other postcards for children to share, compare, and sort.

The chart at right offers an example, at each developmental level, of what children may say and do, along with ideas for scaffolding (supporting and gently extending) children's learning at each level. For additional ideas, refer to the scaffolding chart for Appreciating the Arts on page 36. To read more about scaffolding, see page 20.

Scaffolding Learning at Each Developmental Level

Earlier	Middle	Later
Children may	***Children may***	***Children may***
Focus primarily on nonartistic features; for example, commenting that it's a picture of a dog and then looking for other cards with images of dogs.	Notice one or two artistic features — for example, the medium or a dominant color.	Comment on several artistic qualities — for example, whether the picture shows something real (figurative art) or is just "lines, shapes, and colors" (abstract art); whether something is made of metal or wood; or whether there are lots of lines or broad swaths of color.
Adults can	***Adults can***	***Adults can***
Repeat children's observations and help children look for cards with related images. Extend learning by asking children what else they notice about the picture; for example, the materials used to make it, whether there are background images, or whether the dog is standing in light or shadow.	Ask children what other reproductions feature that medium or have similar (or contrasting) colors. Extend learning by encouraging children to notice additional artistic features; for example, by commenting on the use of "white space" or "illumination" (light) to make an image stand out, and encouraging children to find other reproductions that use the same techniques.	Encourage children to share their cards with others, looking for similarities and differences in the qualities they've mentioned, and talk about variations within a medium — for example, how sculpture can be made of wood, metal, stone, or cloth (fiber). Extend learning by asking children about the artists' intentions and choice of technique: "Why do you think she chose these colors?"

End: When the activity time is up, gather up the cards and let children know where they will be stored, in case they want to continue working with them. Invite children to pretend they are a sculpture made of wood (or metal or cloth) as they move to the next activity in the daily routine.

Follow-up: Post reproductions of artwork at children's eye level throughout the room, choosing pieces that reflect the area in which they are posted; for example, a Mary Cassatt painting of a mother bathing a child in the house area, or a Louise Nevelson wood sculpture in the block area. As you read picture books, find postcards featuring art techniques similar to the illustrations (for example, Milton Avery's broad-brush figures are similar to those in *The Snowy Day,* by Ezra Jack Keats).

4

World Instruments

Summary description: Children explore instruments from different places and cultures around the world.

Time of day: Small-group time

Materials:

♦ Instruments from different locations and cultures that are small enough for children to play; for example: *percussion* instruments to gently hit, such as gourds, rhythm sticks shaped or carved from different materials, maracas with assorted fillings, castanets, cymbals, tambourines, drums of several shapes and sizes, and triangles; *wind* instruments to blow, such as flutes, recorders, kazoos, and shofars (rams' horn); and *string* instruments to pluck and strum, such as ukuleles, guitars, and fiddles (preferably in child sizes — that is, one-half or three-quarters length and width)

♦ Photos of people using different kinds of instruments.

Curriculum content: KDI 44. Appreciating the Arts. *Also:* KDI 41. Music and KDI 48. Predicting

COR Advantage item: Y. Music. *Also:* item CC. Experimenting, predicting, and drawing conclusions

Beginning: Bring in various instruments from different regions and cultures. Encourage families and other staff to contribute and to join the activity. (Elementary school music departments might also be willing to loan more durable instruments.) Pass around photos of people using the instruments. Invite children and family members to talk about the meaning of the instrument(s) in their own homes and communities, where and how they came to own them, who in the family plays them, and when they play them. Say something like "Let's play these instruments and listen to the different sounds they make."

Middle: Try different instruments yourself, and encourage the children to experiment. Play the instruments one at a time and also play two in sequence, to compare them. Encourage children to listen closely to the sounds they produce on the instruments and to those made by others using different instruments.

The chart at right offers an example, at each developmental level, of what children may say and do, along with ideas for scaffolding (supporting and gently extending) children's learning at each level. For additional ideas, refer to the scaffolding chart for Appreciating the Arts on page 36. To read more about scaffolding, see page 20.

Scaffolding Learning at Each Developmental Level

Earlier	Middle	Later
Children may	**Children may**	**Children may**
Play an instrument in one way — for example, bang on a drum or shake a maraca.	Explore two or more instruments in several ways — for example, strumming, shaking, and pounding them.	Explore multiple instruments, comparing how they are made and the sounds they produce.
Adults can	**Adults can**	**Adults can**
Name the instrument and copy and label children's actions. Extend learning by encouraging children to try another action with that instrument or the same action with a different instrument — "What else could you do with the tambourine?" — and by asking children how they think the new action or instrument will sound.	Describe — and encourage children to describe — the various sound effects they create. Extend learning by encouraging children to compare the sounds produced by different instruments, including those which are dissimilar in key ways (e.g., string and percussion) and those which are quite similar but differ in one significant way (e.g., string instruments that differ in size and the number of strings they have).	Comment on the variety of children's musical explorations: "You tried all the drums and you beat them first with your hands and then hard and soft with different drumsticks." Extend learning by asking children how they think the sounds are made ("What did you do to make the sound come out high-pitched?" or "Tell me what to do so the sound comes out with a low pitch") and by trying out children's hypotheses (ideas) and talking with them about the results.

End: As the activity time nears an end, tell children to try one more instrument; then gather up all the instruments and put them away. Have the children move to the next activity in the daily routine like one of the instruments they played. For example, they might move by stretching like a string, clanging parts of their body together like cymbals, or shaking like maracas.

Follow-up: Arrange for the class to attend a children's concert, especially one where musicians talk about their instruments and how they work, and let children listen to and compare the instrument sounds. Invite family members who play instruments to visit the classroom. Play musical selections that include different types of instruments, such as those featuring string quartets, jug bands, marching bands with prominent horn sections, piano sonatas, and so on. Talk with children about the sounds they hear. Plan a small-group time where children make their own instruments (see activity 6 in this chapter).

5

Composing on Music Paper

> **Summary description:** Children look at written music on music (staff) paper and then write their own songs on music paper.
>
> (*Note:* This activity is similar to promoting writing as part of literacy. Children write strings of notes and musical symbols the same way they string together letters and punctuation marks, developing a knowledge of musical notation and the process of composition (Ohman-Rodriguez, 2005).

Time of day: Small-group time

Materials:

◆ Examples of music written on staff paper (sheet music), including songs familiar to the children

◆ Blank sheets of staff paper

◆ Pencils

Curriculum content: KDI 44. Appreciating the Arts. *Also:* KDI 41. Music and KDI 29. Writing

COR Advantage item: Y. Music. *Also:* item R. Writing

Beginning: Show children a page of music and ask them to guess what it says. Explain that composers write songs in musical notation on special music paper, called staff paper, just as authors write the words that appear on the pages of books. Tell children that musicians read these marks (notes) to know what to sing or play on their instruments and that the notes on the bottom of the staff are low sounds, and the notes at the top are high sounds. Give each child a sample of written music with notes (whole, half, and quarter notes indicating "how long to hold it") and a few symbols, such as the bass and the treble clef ("low and high notes"), the repeat symbol ("play or sing again"), and a rest ("pause" or "wait"). Label and describe these notations to the children, using the simple language suggested here. Sing a familiar song (such as "Twinkle, Twinkle, Little Star"), pointing to each note. Give children blank sheets of music paper and pencils, and invite them to "write a song."

Middle: Continue to talk with children about the sheet music, identifying the notes and symbols. Observe and comment on the marks children make on their papers, using the language of musical annotation; for example, you might say, "The note you made on the top line would be sung high, and the note on the bottom line would be sung low." Invite children to "sing" what they have written.

The chart at right offers an example, at each developmental level, of what children may say and do, along with ideas for scaffolding (supporting and gently extending) children's learning at each level. For additional ideas, refer to the scaffolding chart for Appreciating the Arts on page 36. To read more about scaffolding, see page 20.

Scaffolding Learning at Each Developmental Level

Earlier	Middle	Later
Children may	***Children may***	***Children may***
Scribble on the staff paper and say they are writing music, perhaps naming a familiar song: "I'm writing the boat song."	Make circles and vertical lines resembling notes, distributed on the staff paper.	Write many notes and several symbols on the staff paper.
Adults can	***Adults can***	***Adults can***
Say something like "You are writing the notes for 'Row, Row, Row Your Boat.'" Extend learning by looking at and singing that song (or another one children know), pointing out where the notes are placed along the staff as voices go higher and lower; and by pointing out the song's title, where the song begins and ends on the page, how to follow a line of music from left to right, and so on.	Copy children's marks on their own paper, and make a comment like "I'm writing a song like yours"; ask children if their song has a name and, if it does, write it at the top of the page. Extend learning by asking children to teach adults their song by singing and pointing to the notes and symbols on their page; adults can use their finger to follow along as children sing and teach them their song.	Ask children to tell them about what they have written, supplying names if they ask; for example, "The filled-in circle is called a whole note." Extend learning by encouraging children to compare what they have composed to the samples and by asking what other notes or musical notation they could add to their compositions.

End: Close the activity by encouraging children to sing or describe their song to the rest of the group. Collect the staff paper and pencils, and store them where you keep other writing supplies in the classroom. Tell children to "take long steps like whole notes" or "short steps like quarter notes" as they move to the next activity in the daily routine.

Follow-up: Add sheet music of the children's favorite songs to the class songbook. When you sing these songs with children, point to the notes and other musical annotations. Put songbooks with written music in the book area. On the message board, draw "notes" to indicate when the children will be learning a new song at large-group time.

6 *Making Instruments*

Summary description: Children create their own musical instruments and describe how they work.

Time of day: Small-group time (preferably after children have done activity 4 in this chapter, "World Instruments")

Materials:

- Boxes (including ones made of thin cardboard that children can easily cut or poke holes in)
- Yarn, string, and wire of different elasticities and thicknesses
- Objects that can be used for striking, such as sticks, twigs, small blocks, long-handled kitchen utensils (spoons, spatulas)
- Objects that can be used to strum, such as guitar picks, metal bolts, or heavy cardboard rectangles (small enough for children to hold and manipulate using one hand)
- Chain links of different diameters and thicknesses
- Tin cans (cleaned and with sharp edges removed)
- Plastic and metal bottle caps
- Small metal objects such as washers, screws, and paperclips
- Plastic containers and lids
- Combs and brushes
- Tape
- Twist ties (preferably long and thick ties, such as you might find among gardening supplies)

Curriculum content: KDI 44. Appreciating the Arts. *Also:* KDI 41. Music, KDI 4. Problem solving, and KDI 17. Fine-motor skills

COR Advantage item: Y. Music. *Also:* item B. Problem-solving with materials and item J. Fine-motor skills

Beginning: After children are familiar with a variety of instruments and how they produce sounds (see activity 4 in this chapter, "World Instruments"), say something like "Today we're going to make our own musical instruments." Let children explore and talk about the materials on the table. Give each child a basket with several (four to six) materials, including tape, and say "I wonder what instruments you will make."

Middle: Talk about the materials children use and how their instruments work. Encourage children to demonstrate a variety of sounds. Ask if their instrument has a name; accept that they may call it by a familiar name or an invented one. Help children solve problems with materials (for example, how to cut a hole in a box or attach strings) and refer them to one another for assistance.

The chart at right offers examples, at each developmental level, of what children may say and do, along with ideas for scaffolding (supporting and gently extending) learning at each developmental level. For additional ideas, refer to the scaffolding chart for Appreciating the Arts on page 36. To read more about scaffolding, see page 20.

Scaffolding Learning at Each Developmental Level		
Earlier	**Middle**	**Later**
Children may	***Children may***	***Children may***
Play with the materials without making an instrument.	Make simple instruments, such as shakers or drums, with a couple of materials.	Use several materials to make elaborate instruments, such as "guitars" (using boxes, wire, tape, and a bolt for strumming).
Adults can	***Adults can***	***Adults can***
Use the materials in the same way children do and comment on their properties; for example, pointing out that the yarn is stretchy but that the wire is stiff. Extend learning by making sounds with the materials and by encouraging children to imitate and expand on the adults' actions — for example, by putting metal washers in a plastic container, putting on the lid and shaking it, and then handing it to a child to explore.	Ask children how they made their instrument, so they can make one like it. Extend learning by asking children to describe how their instrument makes sounds; wonder aloud how children could move it another way and/or add materials to produce a different sound.	Describe — and ask children to describe — how the children created distinctive sounds: "What did you use to make that clicking noise?" Extend learning by encouraging children to listen to one another's instruments individually and to play them together, comparing their sounds.

End: Ask children to show one another their instruments, then have everyone march around the room playing them. Invite children to add their instruments to the music area or put them in their cubbies to take home. Have them pretend to play an instrument (strumming, banging, blowing, and so on) as they move to the next activity in the routine.

Follow-up: Bring in photos of unusual instruments from around the world (e.g., gourds, flutes) and add these to the music area. Download and play recordings of different instruments, including some that are familiar and some that are new to the children. As children play with materials at work (choice) or outside time, now and then wonder how they could use them to create musical sounds; for example, by dropping small metal objects with a dump truck to make a tinkly noise or rubbing a blade of grass until it squeaks.

7

Dancing Like the Stars

Summary description: After watching and/or reading about a dance performance, children create their own expressive movement pieces.

Time of day: Large-group time, following a field trip and/or reading books about dancing

Note: Here are a few book suggestions: *Dance!* by Bill T. Jones and Susan Kuklin; *Beautiful Ballerina* by Marilyn Nelson and Susan Kuklin; *Happy Feet: The Savoy Lindy Hoppers and Me* by Richard Michelson and E.B. Lewis

Materials:
- Music and music player
- As backup, objects to move with, such as scarves and paper plates
- As backup, dress-up clothes and/or materials and tools to create costumes

Curriculum content:
KDI 44. Appreciating the Arts.
Also: KDI 42. Movement,
KDI 16. Gross-motor skills, and
KDI 18. Body awareness

COR Advantage item: Z. Movement.
Also: item I. Gross-motor skills

Beginning: Take children on a field trip to a dance performance — for example, to see a troupe that gives concerts for children, to a street fair, or to a dance school recital. If it is permitted, take photos or videos. In addition (or if a live performance is not feasible), read illustrated books about dance. The next day, remind children of the trip and/or the books you read. Talk about what they saw, and look at the pictures from the performance and in the books. Play music similar to what they heard and/or read about and say something like "I wonder what kinds of dances you will create."

Middle: Move expressively with the children, sometimes imitating their actions, and occasionally introducing new ideas. Change the music every three minutes or so, playing different genres or emphasizing different qualities, such as the tempo or mood, to elicit varying interpretations. Encourage children to listen to the music before they begin to move.

The chart at right offers an example, at each developmental level, of what children may say and do, along with ideas for scaffolding (supporting and gently extending) children's learning at each level. For additional ideas, refer to the scaffolding chart for Appreciating the Arts on page 36. To read more about scaffolding, see page 20.

Scaffolding Learning at Each Developmental Level

Earlier	Middle	Later
Children may	***Children may***	***Children may***
Start to move without listening to the music; they may move in one way.	Listen to the music for five or ten seconds before they start to move.	Spontaneously comment on the dance performance and how they are trying to imitate the movements they saw; they may identify dance steps they particularly admired.
Adults can	***Adults can***	***Adults can***
Imitate and describe children's movements, saying things like "I'm turning in a circle like you." Extend learning by saying something like "Let's listen to the music — tell me how it sounds to you" and then by encouraging children to move like the descriptive words they use — for example, saying "How could you move in a 'boom, boom' way?"	Describe children's movements and how these match the music's qualities. Extend learning by comparing children's movements to those the children saw at the dance performance: "You're swaying your arms over your head like the ballet dancer" or "You are squatting and kicking your feet in front of you like the Russian folk dancer at the street fair."	Acknowledge the similarities between children's movements and those of the dancers, and encourage children to say why they liked certain movements. Extend learning by asking children to try another type of movement they observed or to do the "opposite" of what the dancers did and by encouraging children to elaborate their dances using props or costumes.

End: Tell the children when you are about to play the last selection. When it is over, have children bow or do whatever action the dancers did at the end of their performance. Have the class clap for itself. Tell the children to dance to the next activity in the daily routine.

Follow-up: Bring in posters and newspaper photos of dance performances. Talk about the stage sets and costumes. If children choose to recreate the field trip during work (choice) time, provide materials and tools to make props, sell tickets, seat the audience, make flashlights for ushers, and so on. Advise families of free and low-cost dance performances suitable to take their children to.

8

Dancing Around the World

> **Summary description:** Children listen and move to a variety of musical selections from around the world and move to the music.

Time of day: Large-group time

Materials:

♦ Musical selections, each lasting about three minutes, representing various genres and regions of the world (see "Incorporating Cultural Diversity in Music" on p. 73. for suggestions)

♦ Music player

♦ As a backup material, photos of people dancing to different types of music, wearing native costumes or ceremonial garments, and celebrating holidays or other occasions

Curriculum content: KDI 44. Appreciating the Arts. *Also:* KDI 41. Music, KDI 16. Gross-motor development, and KDI 53. Diversity

COR Advantage items: Y. Music, and Z. Movement. *Also:* item I. Gross-motor development and item FF. Knowledge of self and others

Beginning: Play a musical selection the children may not have heard before — for example, an Indian raga. Ask children to describe the music, saying something like "What do you hear?" and then encouraging them to move to it. After three minutes, change to a different selection — for example, a Tibetan chant, an Eastern European polka, or Native American flute music. Say "Here's a different kind of music." Ask children to describe what they hear this time (for example, the sounds made by the instruments or the singers' voices). Then say "I wonder how you will move to this music."

Middle: Label (name) the types of music you play. Describe, and encourage children to describe, the characteristics of the different selections and how children are moving to reflect those qualities. Invite discussion about the types of music children listen to with their families and how these resemble or differ from the music they are listening to now. Ask how and when children like to dance at home or in other settings (for example, they may have attended weddings, pow-wows, or an older sibling's recital).

The chart at right offers an example, at each developmental level, of what children may say and do, along with ideas for scaffolding (supporting and gently extending) children's learning at each level. For additional ideas, refer to the scaffolding chart for Appreciating the Arts on page 36. To read more about scaffolding, see page 20.

Scaffolding Learning at Each Developmental Level

Earlier	Middle	Later
Children may	***Children may***	***Children may***
Move the same way to different types of music.	Vary one or two movements to match the music; for example, they may slow down and then speed up, or bounce up and down and then sway side to side.	Move in many ways and ask, "What do you call this music?"
Adults can	***Adults can***	***Adults can***
Imitate and label (name) children's movements. Extend learning by commenting on a quality of the music — for example, by saying "This sounds lively" — and moving in a way that reflects that quality; seeing if the children imitate, while accepting their choice if they don't; and by asking children how the music sounds to them and wondering aloud how they could move that way: "How could you move fast?"	Describe — and encourage children to describe — children's movements. Extend learning by asking children to explain what about the music made them choose to move that way.	Name the type of music and say something about where it comes from or how people dance to it: "This is ballet — people wear special costumes and dance on tiptoe to this music." Extend learning by sharing photos of various groups dancing to the different types of music.

End: Tell children when you are about to play the last selection. Encourage them to pay attention to the different ways in which they and their peers move to express its qualities. Continue to play the final musical selection as children transition to the next activity in the daily routine.

Follow-up: Repeat this activity using handheld instruments (e.g., maracas, finger cymbals) and other objects children can move with (e.g., scarves, paper plates). Continue to play a wide variety of music to move to at large-group time. Encourage families to bring in recordings and show the children simple dance steps. Visit street fairs where dancers perform to different types of music.

9

Mime

Summary description: Children use mime (body gestures and facial expressions only) to act out real and imaginary scenarios.

Time of day: Large-group time

Materials:
None

Curriculum content: KDI 44. Appreciating the Arts. *Also:* KDI 43. Pretend Play and KDI 9. Emotions

COR Advantage item: AA. Pretend Play. *Also:* item D. Emotions

Beginning: Tell children there is a kind of pretend play called "mime" in which actors use only gestures and facial expressions — no talking or other sounds — to act out situations. Demonstrate this — for example, act out being tired and going to sleep (yawn, stretch, rub your eyes, lie down, pretend to plump up the pillows and cover yourself with a blanket.) Ask the children to suggest something else to mime and act it out together. Ask "What else could we mime?"

Middle: Continue to get children's suggestions for things to mime and ideas on how to do it. Encourage them to observe and imitate one another and to offer their own ideas. Comment on their body positions and facial expressions, and ask what they represent. For example, you might say, "What are you feeling when you scrunch up your face?" After the children have acted out familiar situations, encourage them to invent imaginary ones from favorite books or pretend play scenarios. Remind them that, unlike their regular pretend play, they can't use words when they mime.

The chart at right offers an example, at each developmental level, of what children may say and do, along with ideas for scaffolding (supporting and gently extending) children's learning at each level. For additional ideas, refer to the scaffolding chart for Appreciating the Arts on page 36. To read more about scaffolding, see page 20.

Scaffolding Learning at Each Developmental Level

Earlier	Middle	Later
Children may	***Children may***	***Children may***
Copy the positions and expressions of others, occasionally accompanying them with words or sounds.	Mime familiar scenarios, such as those they enact during pretend play (e.g., soothing a crying baby, getting a shot at the doctor's office, crashing a car into a tower, or steering a truck).	Enact multistep mimes of both familiar and imaginary situations.
Adults can	***Adults can***	***Adults can***
Imitate children's movements, but without speaking. Extend learning by encouraging children to act out their ideas using only their bodies and faces: "I wonder how you could show you're angry without growling."	Acknowledge and carry out children's ideas, and encourage other children to copy and elaborate on their ideas. Extend learning by suggesting that children think of a scene in a favorite book and reenact it without words: "How could you act out something that happened to Alexander during his terrible, horrible, no good, very bad day?"	Guess what children are depicting. Extend learning by having children guess what an adult is miming, and ask what body movements or facial expressions "clued" them in; continue to take turns with children miming and guessing scenarios; encourage children to guess one another's mimes.

End: Ask the children to suggest one more mime and to think of all the ways they can act it out. Choose a scenario (such as sleepwalking, riding a tricycle, or crossing a river on stepping stones) and have children mime it as they move to the next activity.

Follow-up: Instead of giving verbal directions, occasionally mime instructions and have children guess what you are asking them to do. During message board, act out rather than write a message, and have children guess what it is. Mime favorite storybooks, songs, and nursery rhymes.

10   *The Play's the Thing*

> **Summary description:** After a field trip to watch a play (or building on children's family experience of seeing a movie or show), children act out the experience of going to the theater.

Time of day: Large-group time, following a field trip or children's reported family experiences

Materials:

♦ Props to make tickets, chairs, a stage, lights (flashlights), a curtain, and so on

♦ Dress-up clothes

♦ Materials and tools to create additional props such as boxes, blocks, paper, crayons, tape

Curriculum content: KDI 44. Appreciating the Arts. *Also:* KDI 43. Pretend Play and KDI 22. Speaking

COR Advantage item: AA. Pretend Play. *Also:* item L. Speaking

Beginning: Take a field trip to see a live performance of a play created for a children's audience. Alternatively, invite a community theater group to the classroom. Arrange for the children to see and talk with the staff and cast about such things as ticket-taking, stage sets, costumes, lighting, and the characters in the story. (If attending a live performance as a class is not feasible, build on children's family experiences of going to a show or to the movies.) The next day at large-group time, say something like "Yesterday when we got to the theater (or when you went to the show with your family), the first thing we did was hand in our tickets. How should we act that out?"

Middle: Continue to recall the trip in sequence, focusing on all aspects of the theater experience, not just the story of the play. For example, act out being led to the seats by an usher, sitting in the theater as the lights go down, watching the curtain open, looking at the sets and costumes, and applauding when the performance is over. Encourage children to recall details of what they saw and did and to incorporate props such as paper tickets, rows of chairs with an "aisle" down the middle, a curtain (sheet or blanket), and house lights or stage lighting (flashlights).

The chart at right offers an example, at each developmental level, of what children may say and do, along with ideas for scaffolding (supporting and gently extending) children's learning at each level. For additional ideas, refer to the scaffolding chart for Appreciating the Arts on page 36. To read more about scaffolding, see page 20.

Scaffolding Learning at Each Developmental Level

Earlier	Middle	Later
Children may	***Children may***	***Children may***
Act out the events the teacher recalls, looking to their peers for guidance on what to do.	Recall parts of the theater experience on their own.	Use movements, gestures, and props to reenact parts of the field trip that were meaningful to them.
Adults can	***Adults can***	***Adults can***
Refer children to others for ideas: "Ali is making a row of chairs like the seats at the theater — it looks like he could use some help." Extend learning by asking what else children recall about specific things they saw and did: "The seats were really soft. What else do you remember about the seats?"	Acknowledge children's ideas and encourage others to act them out: "Sofia says it got really dark and then the curtain went up; how should we show that?" Extend learning by helping children fill in the sequence of events: "Something happened on the stage before that. Do you remember what it was?"	Ask children what else they could do or use to represent their experiences: "What else was the farmer wearing? What could we use for that?" Extend learning by introducing vocabulary words about the theater, such as *director* and *actor, set* and *costume, lighting, script, rehearsal, curtain call,* and *applause* (for the latter, possibly saying, "It means to clap").

End: Bring group time to a close by having the children pretend to return to school by whatever means of transportation you used on the field trip. Have them pretend to use that same form of transportation as they transition to the next activity in the daily routine.

Follow-up: Provide props and materials for children who want to pretend "going to the theater" during work (choice) time. Do another theater reenactment, this time focusing on the narrative (story) of the play the children saw. Tell families about low-cost and free opportunities to attend community theater events designed for children. Incorporate elements of the theater into planning and recall; for example, put objects representing each area behind a "curtain" that children can bring "on stage" as they describe what they will do, or did, at work time.

References

Bayless, K. M., & Ramsey, M. E. (2004). *Music: A way of life for the young child*. Upper Saddle River, NJ: Prentice Hall.

Bodrova, E., & Leong, D. J. (2005). Promoting student self–regulation in learning. *Education Digest, 71*(2), 54–57.

Bodrova, E., & Leong, D. (2007). *Tools of the mind: The Vygotskian approach to early childhood education* (2nd ed.). New York, NY: Prentice Hall.

Bradley, K. K. (2002). Informing and reforming dance education research. In R. J. Deasy (Ed.), *Critical links: Learning in the arts and student academic and social development* (pp. 27–29). ERIC Number: ED466413. Download at http://eric.ed.gov/?id=ED466413

Bruner, J. S. (1986). *Actual minds, possible worlds*. Cambridge, MA: Harvard University Press.

Burton, J. (2000). The configuration of meaning: Learner–centered art education revisited. *Studies in Art Education, 41*(4), 330–342.

Catterall, J. S. (2002a). The arts and transfer of learning. In R. J. Deasy (Ed.) *Critical links: Learning in the arts and student academic and social development* (pp. 162–168). ERIC document number: ED466413. Download at http://eric.ed.gov/?id=ED466413

Catterall, J. S. (2002b). Research on drama and theater in education. In R. J. Deasy (Ed.) *Critical links: Learning in the arts and student academic and social development* (pp. 69–73). ERIC document number: ED466413. Download at http://eric.ed.gov/?id=ED466413

Centers for Disease Control. (2010). *The association between school–based physical activity, including physical education, and academic performance*. Atlanta, GA: US Department of Health and Human Services.

Cheatham, G. A., & Ro, Y. E. (2010). Young English learners' interlanguage as a context for language and early literacy development. *Young Children, 65*(4), 18–23.

Chenfeld, M. B. (2005). Education is a moving experience: Get movin'! In D. Koralek (Ed.). *Spotlight on young children and the creative arts* (pp. 50–51). Washington, DC: National Association for the Education of Young Children.

Copple, C., & Bredekamp, S. (Eds.). (2009). *Developmentally appropriate practice in early childhood programs serving children from birth through age 8* (3rd ed.). Washington, DC: National Association for the Education of Young Children.

Creasey, G. L., Jarvis, P. A., & Berk, L. E. (1998). Play and social competence. In O. N. Saracho & B. Spodek (Eds.), *Multiple perspectives on play in early childhood education* (pp. 116–143). Albany, NY: State University of New York.

Deasy, R., & Stevenson, L. (2002). *The arts: Critical links to student success*. Washington, DC: Arts Education Partnership, Council of Chief State School Officers.

Dewar, G. (2013). The social world of newborns: A guide for the science–minded parent. *Parenting Science*. Retrieved from http://www.parentingscience.com/newborns–and–the–social–world.html.

Dewey, J. (1934). *Art as experience.* New York, NY: Perigee Books.

Dow, C. B. (2010). Young children and movement: The power of creative dance. *Young Children, 65*(2), 30–35.

Drew, W. F., & Rankin, B. (2005). Promoting creativity for life using open–ended materials. In D. Koralek (Ed.), *Spotlight on young children and the creative arts* (pp. 32–39). Washington, DC: National Association for the Education of Young Children.

Epstein, A. S. (2005). Thinking about art: Encouraging art appreciation in early childhood settings. In D. Koralek (Ed.), *Spotlight on young children and the creative arts* (pp. 52–57). Washington, DC: National Association for the Education of Young Children.

Epstein, A. S. (2012). *The HighScope Preschool Curriculum: Creative arts.* Ypsilanti, MI: HighScope Press.

Epstein, A. S., & Hohmann, M. (2012). *The HighScope Preschool Curriculum.* Ypsilanti, MI: HighScope Press.

Epstein, A. S., & Trimis, E. (2002). *Supporting young artists: The development of the visual arts in young children.* Ypsilanti, MI: HighScope Press.

Francois, C., Chobert, J., Besson, M., & Schon, D. (2013). Music training for the development of speech segmentation. *Cerebral Cortex, 23*(9), 2038–2043. doi: 10.1093/cercor/bhs180

Friedman, S. (2010). Theater, live music, and dance: Conversations about young audiences. *Young Children 65*(2), 36–41.

Gardner, H. (1990). *Art education and human development.* Los Angeles, CA: Getty Center for Education in the Arts.

Geist, K., Geist, E. A., & Kuznik, K. (2012). The patterns of music: Young children learning mathematics through beat, rhythm, and melody. *Young Children, 67*(1), 74–79.

Gelman, S. A., & Opfer, J. E. (2002). Development of the animate–inanimate distinction. In U. Goswami (Ed.), *Blackwell handbook of childhood cognitive development* (pp. 151–166). Malden, MA: Blackwell.

Greata, J. (2006). *An introduction to music in early childhood education.* Clifton Park, NY: Delmar Learning.

Horowitz, R., & Webb–Dempsey, J. (2002). Promising signs of positive effects: Lessons from the multi–arts studies. In R. J. Deasy (Ed.), *Critical links: Learning in the arts and student academic and social development* (pp. 109–111). ERIC document number: ED466413.

Kavanaugh, R. D. (2006). Pretend play. In B. Spodek & O. N. Saracho (Eds.), *Handbook of research on the education of young children* (2nd ed., pp. 269–278). Mahwah, NJ: Lawrence Erlbaum.

Kemple, K. M., Batey, J., & Hartle, L. (2005). Music play: Creating centers for musical play and exploration. In D. Koralek (Ed.). *Spotlight on young children and the creative arts* (pp. 24–31). Washington, DC: National Association for the Education of Young Children.

Kim, J., & Robinson, H. M. (2010). Four steps for becoming familiar with early music standards. *Young Children, 65*(2), 42–47.

Kindler, A. M. (1995). Significance of adult input in early childhood artistic development. In C. M. Thompson (Ed.), *The visual arts and early childhood learning* (pp. 1–5). Reston, VA: National Art Education Association.

Koralek, D. (2005). Introduction. In D. Koralek (Ed.), *Spotlight on young children and the creative arts* (pp. 2–3). Washington, DC: National Association for the Education of Young Children.

Koralek, D. (2010). Introduction—Interview with Mimi Brodsky Chenfeld. *Young Children, 65*(2), 10–12.

LaMore, R., Root–Bernstein, R., Root–Bernstein, M., Schweitzer, J. H., Lawton, J. L., Roraback, E., Peruski, A., VanDyke, M., & Fernandez, L. (2013). Arts and crafts: Critical to economic innovation. *Economic Development Quarterly, 27*(3), 221–229. doi:10.1177/0891242413486186

Leong, D., & Bodrova, E. (2012). Assessing and scaffolding make–believe play. *Young Children, 67*(1), 28–34.

Marigliano, M. L., & Russo, M. J. 2011. Foster preschoolers' critical thinking and problem solving through movement. *Young Children, 66*(5), 44–49.

Matlock, R., & Hornstein, J. (2005). Saber–toothed tiger: Learning and the arts through the ages. In D. Koralek (Ed.), *Spotlight on young children and the creative arts* (pp. 6–11). Washington, DC: National Association for the Education of Young Children.

Maynard, C., & Ketter, K. J. (2013). The value of open–ended art. *Teaching young children, 7*(1), 24–27.

Mitchell, L. C. (2005). Making the MOST of creativity in activities for young children with disabilities. In D. Koralek (Ed.), *Spotlight on young children and the creative arts* (pp. 40–43). Washington, DC: National Association for the Education of Young Children.

National Art Education Association. (2006). *Art: Essential for early learning* (position paper of the Early Childhood Art Educators Issues Group). Reston, VA: Author.

Ohman–Rodriguez, J. (2005). Music from inside out: Promoting emergent composition with young children. In D. Koralek (Ed.), *Spotlight on young children and the creative arts* (pp. 44–49). Washington, DC: National Association for the Education of Young Children.

Paley, V. (1981). *Wally's stories.* Cambridge, MA: Harvard University Press.

Parsons, M. J. (1987). *How we understand art.* Cambridge, UK: Cambridge University.

Piaget, J. (1926/1959). *The language and thought of the child.* New York: Humanities Press.

Pica, R. (2009). Make a little music. *Young Children, 64*(6), 74–75.

Pica, R. (2011). Taking movement education outdoors. *Young Children, 66*(4), 58–59.

Pinciotti, P. (2006). Changing lenses: It's all about art! In B. Neugebauer (Ed.), *Curriculum — Art, music, movement, drama: A beginnings workshop book* (pp 11–14). Redmond, WA: Exchange.

Prairie, A. P. (2013). Supporting sociodramatic play in ways that enhance academic learning. *Young Children, 68*(2), 62–68.

Rabinowich, T–C., Cross, I., & Burnard, P. (2013). Long–term musical group interaction has a positive influence on empathy in young children. *Psychology of Music, 41*(4), 484–498. doi: 10.1177/0305735612440609

Ratey, J. J. (2008). *SPARK: The revolutionary new science of exercise and the brain*. New York, NY: Little Brown.

Root–Bernstein, M. (2014). *Inventing imaginary worlds: From childhood play to adult creativity across the arts and science*. Washington, DC: Rowan & Littlefield.

Rosengren, K. S. & Hickling, A. K. (2000). The development of children's thinking about possible events and plausible mechanisms. In K. S. Rosengren, C. N. Johnson, & P. L. Harris (Eds.), *Imagining the possible* (pp. 75–98). Cambridge: Cambridge University Press.

Rubin, K. H., Bukowski, W., & Parker, J. (2006). Peer interactions, relationships, and groups. In N. Eisenberg (Ed.), *Handbook of child psychology, Vol. 3: Social, emotional, and personality development* (6th ed., pp. 571–645). New York, NY: John Wiley & Sons.

Sawyers, K. S. (with Colley, E., & Icaza, L.). (2010). *Moving with purpose: 54 activities for learning, fitness, and fun*. Ypsilanti, MI: HighScope Press.

Schiller, M. (1995). An emergent art curriculum that fosters understanding. *Young Children, 50*(3), 33–38.

Scott–Kasner, C. (1992). Research on music in early childhood. In R. Colwell (Ed.), *Handbook of research on music teaching and learning* (pp. 633–650). Reston, VA: Music Educators National Conference.

Scripp, L. (2002). An overview of research on music and learning. In R. J. Deasy (Ed.), *Critical links: Learning in the arts and student academic and social development* (pp. 143–147). ERIC Number: ED466413. Download at http://eric.ed.gov/?id=ED466413

Sims, W. L. (1985). Young children's creative movement to music: Categories of movement, rhythmic characteristics, and reactions to change. *Contributions to Music Education, 12*, 42–50.

Sobel, D. (2001). *Galileo's daughter: A historical memoir of science, faith, and love*. New York, NY: Walker and Company.

Sobel, D. M. (2006). How fantasy benefits young children's understanding of pretense. *Developmental Science, 9*, 63–75.

Soundy, C. S., & Lee, Y. H. (2013). A medley of pictures and patterns in children's drawings. *Young Children, 68*(2), 70–77.

Sousa, D. A. (2006). How the arts develop the young brain. *The School Administrator, 63*(11), 19–24. Retrieved from http://www.aasa.org/School-AdministratorArticle.aspx?id=7378

Spodek, B. (2008). Educationally appropriate art activities for young children. In *Curriculum: Art, music, movement, drama — A Beginnings Workshop book* (pp. 13–16). Redmond, WA: Exchange Press.

Stellaccio, C. K., & McCarthy, M. (1999). Research in early childhood music and movement education. In C. Seefeldt (Ed.), *The early childhood curriculum: Current findings in theory and practice* (3rd ed., pp. 179–200). New York, NY: Teachers College Press.

Subbotsky, E. V. (2004). Magical thinking in judgments of causation: Can anomalous phenomenon affect ontological causal beliefs in children and adults? *British Journal of Developmental Psychology, 22*, 123–152.

Swann, A. C. (2008). Children, objects, and relations: Constructivist foundation in the Reggio Emilia approach. *Studies in art education, 50*(1), 36–50.

Tabors, P. O. (2008). *One child, two languages: A guide for preschool educators of children learning English as a second language.* Baltimore, MD: Brookes.

Tarr, P. (2008, July). New visions: Art for early childhood. *Art Education, 61*(4), 19–24.

Taunton, M., & Colbert, M. (2000). Art in the early childhood classroom: Authentic experiences and extended dialogues. In N. J. Yelland (Ed.), *Promoting meaningful learning: Innovation in educating early childhood professionals* (pp. 67–76). Washington, DC: National Association for the Education of Young Children.

Tierney, A., & Kraus, N. (2013). The ability to move to a beat is linked to the consistency of neural responses to sound. *The Journal of Neuroscience, 33*(38), 14981–14988.

Vygotsky, L. S. (1978) *Mind and society: The development of higher psychological processes.* Cambridge, MA: Harvard University Press.

Wanerman, T. (2010). Using story drama with young preschoolers. *Young Children, 65*(2), 20–28.

Wien, C. A., Keating, B–L., & Bigelow, B. (2008). Moving into uncertainty: Sculpture with three–to–five–year–olds. *Young Children, 63*(4), 78–86.

Wardle, F., & Cruz–Janzen, M. I. (2004). *Meeting the needs of multiethnic and multiracial children in schools.* Boston, MA: Allyn and Bacon.

Weikart, P. S. (2000). *Round the circle: Key experiences in movement for young children* (2nd ed.). Ypsilanti, MI: HighScope Press.

West, N. T. (2005). Art for all children: A conversation about inclusion. *Exchange, 27*(5), 47–51.

Wien, C. A. (with Keating, B–L. & Bigelow, B.). (2008). Moving into uncertainty: Sculpture with three–to–five–year–olds. *Young Children, 63*(4), 78–86.

Wright, S. (2003). *The arts, young children, and learning.* Boston, MA: Pearson.

Appendix: How to Use the Scaffolding Charts in This Book

Scaffolding is an essential component of early education because young children develop along a continuum; children, even those at the same chronological age, vary in their development and ability levels. Scaffolding charts acknowledge this variability and help you foster learning for all children, including dual language learners (DLLs) and those with special needs.

Each of the activities in this book includes a scaffolding chart that contains suggestions for supporting and extending children's learning in an identified content area. These scaffolding charts are meant to be a guide to possible content-related learning. However, you should expect that children will use materials in unique ways and be ready to support whatever learning may take place.

Each scaffolding chart is divided into three columns with the headings "Earlier," "Middle," and "Later," which contain examples of what young children at these three developmental levels might do and say (related to the designated content area) as they engage with the materials and/or in the activity. For each of these three developmental stages, each chart includes a section called "Adults can," which offers examples of how you can support and gently extend learning at the three developmental levels as you interact with children during the activity.

To scaffold children's learning for any given activity in this book, you can follow these three steps:

Step 1. Consider children's developmental levels.

Look at the scaffolding chart for the activity and carefully read through what children might say or do at each developmental level. Anticipate how the individual children in your small group or your classroom might respond to this activity — that is, which children might respond at an earlier, middle, or later developmental level, and how they might use the provided materials. This will help you think more intentionally about the different ways you will need to interact with children, depending on their levels of development (Step 2).

Step 2. Provide support at children's current level of development.

Once you have a picture of what children might do during the activity, you can plan how you will support their current levels of development. Look under "Adults can…" on the activity scaffolding chart for ideas on how to support each child's current level of development. These might include strategies such as imitating and labeling the child's actions, intentionally using content-related vocabulary to describe what the child is doing, or asking the child to describe what he or she is doing. As a strategy, remember to pause to see how the child responds to your overtures. This will give you clues about whether to continue with Step 2 or move on to Step 3.

Step 3. Offer gentle extensions.

If children respond eagerly to your support strategies, you may try introducing a new idea within the context of what they are doing. Look at the paragraphs in the "Adults can" section that begin "Extend learning by…." These paragraphs include strategies for extending children's learning in the specific content area — such as drawing attention to another child's actions by making a comment, asking the child to explain his or her thinking, gently introducing a new concept or idea, or posing a challenge.

By following these steps as you use the activity scaffolding charts, you can encourage children's development and expand the possibilities inherent in each activity for each chil

About the Author

Dr. Ann S. Epstein, formerly Senior Director of Curriculum Development at HighScope Educational Research Foundation, retired in 2015 after working at the foundation for more than 40 years. Her areas of expertise include curriculum development, professional development, research and program evaluation, and instrument development. Dr. Epstein's publications include *The Intentional Teacher; Essentials of Active Learning in Preschool; The HighScope Preschool Curriculum; Me, You, Us: Social-Emotional Learning in Preschool; Numbers Plus Preschool Mathematics Curriculum; Tender Care and Early Learning: Supporting Infants and Toddlers in Child Care Settings; Supporting Young Artists;* and *Small-Group Times to Scaffold Early Learning.* She was also a key developer of COR Advantage, HighScope's observational assessment of children from infancy through kindergarten, and the Program Quality Assessment (PQA), HighScope's tool for measuring teaching practices and program management. In addition to a PhD in developmental psychology, Dr. Epstein has a Masters of Fine Arts degree and has had her artwork exhibited, and works of fiction, published.